W9-BHF-453

I'm Studying Reading!

Book D

Perfection Learning®

© 2001 Perfection Learning Corporation
1000 North Second Avenue, P. O. Box 500, Logan, Iowa 51546-0500

78952 ISBN 0-7891-5416-1
Printed in the U.S.A.

Design: Lynda Banks Design
Cover and Inside Illustration: Michael A. Aspengren
Cover Design: Jan Michalson

How to Be a Reading Whiz

Reading is the fastest way to get smart, especially school smart.

For example, if you plan to visit the moon someday, you'd better read a book about it first. At least you'll know what to wear to be a moonwalker! Even if you don't plan a moon trip, a book at hand is the best thing to have on any trip, or anywhere else. Books are the smart way to learn as well as the smart way to beat boredom, especially if you pick exciting books to read. The more you read, the better you read, and the smarter you get.

Unfortunately, you can't always read just those things you like. Sometimes you must read a tough science chapter or a dull story. But if you read a lot, you'll get smart fast, and soon you'll read the boring stuff as fast as the interesting stuff. You'll whiz through science, social studies, and standardized tests, leaving you lots of time for the exciting books you want to read.

To become a reading whiz, you need to learn a reading trick or two. That's what this book will teach you. *I'm Studying Reading!* will make you a smart reader three ways by teaching you to

1. make smart guesses when you stumble on words you don't recognize,

2. make better use of what you already know,

3. and boost your test scores.

It's all done in ten lessons. Each lesson starts with a FOCUS that tells you what you'll learn. Next come learning TASKS and their FEEDBACK. You'll do each Task, then read the Feedback to check your answers. A RECAP signals the end of a lesson and the beginning of a short TEST. The Test will help you practice exactly the skills you need to score well on your school's standardized tests.

Come on! Become a Reading Whiz and get great grades!

Contents

1 Sounds and Letters

Recognizing tricky sounds and letters

> Words with **gh** in them can be tricky.
> Does **enough** look like **enuff**?
> Does **tough** look like **tuff**?
> When you have a cold, do you **cough**?

Task 1

First read the sentence. Then circle the word that <u>rhymes</u> with the underlined word.

1. The meat was too <u>tough</u> to chew.

   go   stuff   tug   bought

2. The cake was good, and I had <u>enough</u> of it.

   go   caught   though   puff

Sometimes **gh** sounds like **ff**.

👉 **Feedback** In one, *tou<u>gh</u>* goes with *stuff. Enou<u>gh</u>* and *puff* rhyme.

> In some words, **gh** helps **tho<u>ught</u>** rhyme with **ca<u>ught</u>**, **thr<u>ough</u>** with **sh<u>oe</u>**, and **altho<u>ugh</u>** with **g<u>o</u>**.

Task 2

Read the sentence and circle the word that rhymes with the underlined word.

1. I played, <u>although</u> I was too small for the team.

   cough   laugh   snow   chew

2. I <u>thought</u> about you today.

   cough   though   taught   pour

3. He came <u>through</u> the door.

   chew   though   thought   enough

Look at the many sounds of **ough**!

👉 **Feedback** In these sentences, **gh** is part of the vowel sound, **ough**. In one, *altho<u>ugh</u>* rhymes with *snow*. In two, *tho<u>ught</u>* goes with *taught*. In three *thr<u>ough</u>* goes with *chew*.

If **c** can sound like **k**,
Then what do you say
When the letters you see
Are **ci**, **cy**, and **ce**?

 Task 3

Circle the word that has the same sound as the underlined letter or letters. Number one is done for you.

1. **<u>c</u>ookie**   cent   city   face   (back)

2. **Ja<u>ck</u>**   cattle   dance   child   cent

3. **<u>k</u>itten**   cookie   face   city   cent

4. **<u>c</u>an**   lace   mice   tick   race

👉 **Feedback** In two, **ck** in *Ja<u>ck</u>* has the same sound as **c** in *<u>c</u>attle*. In three, the **k** in *<u>k</u>itten* has the same sound as the **c** and **k** in *<u>c</u>oo<u>k</u>ie*. The **c** in *fa<u>c</u>e*, *<u>c</u>ity*, and *<u>c</u>ent* all sound like **s** because they have **i** or **e** after them. In four, *<u>c</u>an* and *ti<u>ck</u>* have the same sound.

 Task 4

In this little story, underline the words that have the letter **c** that sounds like **s**.

Prince Carl was racing to school. He was late. It was ice cold and his face was red. He took a short cut and jumped over a fence. The lace on his shoe was loose, and his shoe fell off. Poor Prince Carl had icy toes.

ce, **ci**, **cy**
in <u>c</u>ent,
ra<u>c</u>ing, <u>c</u>ycle

👉 **Feedback** In this story eight words have **c**s with an **s** sound spelled with a **ce**, **ci**, or **cy**. *Prince, racing, ice, face, fence, lace, Prince, icy*.

Most **g** words you know are like
go, **game**, **get**, **give**, and **girl**.
But when you see **ge** and **gi**, the **g** can sound like **j**:
giant, an**ge**l, a**ge**, imag**i**ne.

Sometimes the **g** is hooked to other letters, as in **gn**at,
and becomes silent, just like the **k** in **kn**ow or **kn**ee.

Task 5

Circle the word that has the same sound as the underlined letter.

1. **j**ack   gone   game   giraffe   ago

2. **j**ewel   give   page   gas   grow

3. sa**g**   stage   again   angel   imagine

> Different sounds of **g**

☞ **Feedback** In one, the **g** in *gone*, *game*, and *ago* do not
have *e* or *i* after them. But the *gi* in *giraffe* sounds like the *j* in *jack*.
In two and three, *jewel* and *page* have the *j* sound, and *sag* and *again*
have the same *g* sound.

Task 6

Read this story and circle all the words that use **gn** and **kn**
to make the **n** sound.

On her knees, Audrey was smaller than her dog. Kneeling
near the big animal, she said, "I know you ate this morning,
but I want you to eat more." While she cut more food with
her knife, the dog gnawed on a bone.

Audrey got off of her knees when someone knocked on
the door.

☞ **Feedback** In this story, did you circle *knees*, *Kneeling*, *know*,
knife, *gnawed*, *knees*, *knocked*? The **kn** and **gn** words are tricks that
tests can play on you.

The letter **w** is silent in front of **r**.
That makes **write** sound like **right**.
You're right if you put a **w** before the **r**
when you write the word **write**.
You're **wrong** if you don't.

Task 7

Circle the right **wr** word.

1. On holidays we buy presents and _____ them in pretty paper.

    wreck   wrap   wrestle   wring

2. The man used a _____ to make the bolt tight.

    wriggle   wrist   write   wrench

3. I put my watch on my _____

    wring.   winkle.   wrist.   wreck.

The sound
of **wr**

4. You can get this question right or _____

    wrong.   write.   wrap.   wrist.

☞ **Feedback** You *wrap* presents, use a *wrench* to tighten bolts, and wear a watch on your *wrist*. And you might get answers *wrong* sometimes.

What a funny letter **r** is!
It makes vowels **a**, **e**, **i**, **o**, and **u** sound funny.
If you put **r** after the vowel,
you make **but** into someone's name, **Burt**.

Task 8

Circle the right word.

1. Please come to my birthday _____

    pirty.   purty.   party.   perty.

2. My teacher's apple had a _____ in it.

    worm   warm   worn   werm

A vowel
plus **r** can
make different
sounds.

3. Her _____ was beating loudly.

    hart   heart   hurt   hear

☞ **Feedback** The answers are *party*, *worm*, *heart*.

Task 9 Read each sentence and then circle the word that rhymes with the underlined word.

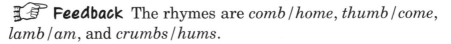

1. You <u>comb</u> your hair in the morning.

   come   home   some   lamb

2. You have four fingers and a <u>thumb</u>.

   come   home   comb   lamb

3. A baby sheep is a <u>lamb</u>.

   comb   dumb   am   and

4. Broken crackers make <u>crumbs</u>.

   homes   hums   comb   lambs

☞ **Feedback** The rhymes are *comb / home*, *thumb / come*, *lamb / am*, and *crumbs / hums*.

The star of the party was Marco. It was his birthday. He went to his bedroom to comb his hair. When he went downstairs, he saw his mother carve his birthday cake.

"All the kids will share this cake," said his mom. "I made this cake, and I did not burn it. It looks good and it is warm."

Marco's little sister, Muffet, climbed on a chair. She stuck her thumb in the cake and ate the crumbs from her thumb.

"Mmm. That's good," she said. Then she put her thumb back in the cake and said, "My thumb wants to learn by heart to make a cake as good as this."

Task 10 Words with **mb** in them can be tricky. Read the story and then answer the questions.

1. What does Marco do to his hair?

   wets it   combs it   eats it   loses it

2. What does his mother do to the cake?

   eats it   gives it to his sister   burns it   carves it

☞ **Feedback** Marco *combs* his hair; his mother *carves* the cake.

A Silly Game of Sounds

Bed, **said**, and **head** don't look the same,
Why do we play this silly game?
May, **day**, **say**, and **way**, and **play**
Look alike but rhyme with **weigh**.

I like to say **you**, **shoe**, **true**, **threw**,
But when I read, can I get **through**
This silly game that is too **rough**?
When I see **though**, I cry, "**Enough**!"

"**No more**!" I say and then I **see**
An **oar** or **four** down by the **sea**.
Let me spell *oar* without *a*, and I **would**
Eat all the oar **wood** if I **could**.

When **write** is **right** I ring a bell
But when I read **wrong** I can't tell
Just why the **r** is not **enough**.
This game for me is far too **tough**.

If **ea** in **beat** and **neat** and **heat**
Sounds just the same as **ee** in **street**
Then how do words like **eat** and **bread**
Not sound the same when they are **said**?

Oh, no! Here's **throw** and **go** and **toe**
I think I've had **enough although**
I can't call "**Whoa**!" until it's **time**
For **off** and **cough** to make a **rhyme**.

Who made this silly alphabet
Where **phone** and **flown** and **Joan** all get
Same sounds, but have such different looks?
I'd rather read a zillion books!

See how much you've learned. Take this test.

Questions 1–15. Look at the key word. One or more letters are underlined. Find the word that has the same sound as the underlined letters. Fill in the circle beside the answer you choose.

1. for
   - Ⓐ over
   - Ⓑ rough
   - Ⓒ even
   - Ⓓ always

2. show
   - Ⓐ allow
   - Ⓑ taught
   - Ⓒ chew
   - Ⓓ though

3. shoe
   - Ⓐ through
   - Ⓑ toe
   - Ⓒ tone
   - Ⓓ although

4. chicken
   - Ⓐ dance
   - Ⓑ cent
   - Ⓒ school
   - Ⓓ place

5. truck
   - Ⓐ chill
   - Ⓑ miss
   - Ⓒ saying
   - Ⓓ scare

6. gym
   - Ⓐ gaggle
   - Ⓑ gorilla
   - Ⓒ game
   - Ⓓ giant

7. gnaw
   - Ⓐ gone
   - Ⓑ grow
   - Ⓒ glaring
   - Ⓓ photo

8. kneel
   - Ⓐ keeper
   - Ⓑ camel
   - Ⓒ kettle
   - Ⓓ sign

9. riding
   - Ⓐ part
   - Ⓑ knowing
   - Ⓒ wrinkles
   - Ⓓ winding

10. bomb
   - Ⓐ bubble
   - Ⓑ coming
   - Ⓒ cable
   - Ⓓ baby

11. turn
   - Ⓐ short
   - Ⓑ sure
   - Ⓒ tuner
   - Ⓓ training

12. call
   - Ⓐ cook
   - Ⓑ thought
   - Ⓒ pal
   - Ⓓ candy

13. giraffe
   - Ⓐ given
   - Ⓑ girls
   - Ⓒ again
   - Ⓓ jewel

14. sat
   - Ⓐ laugh
   - Ⓑ date
   - Ⓒ again
   - Ⓓ always

15. grow
   - Ⓐ enough
   - Ⓑ through
   - Ⓒ though
   - Ⓓ cough

STOP

Number Correct/Total=_____ /15

2 Word Analysis

Recognizing compound words, base words, and word endings

When two little words are put together
to make one word,
the new word is called a **compound word**.
Bobcat is a compound word.
A **bobcat** is a **wildcat** with a **bobtail**.

bob + cat   **wild + cat**   **bob + tail**

Task 1

Circle the missing part of the compound word.
The first one is done for you.

1. My pet elephant loves pea _____   tubs.   boys.   (nuts.)

2. Eva likes to feel _____ drops.   rain   birth   mail

3. Farmer Dorp ate the jelly _____   work.   brush.   beans.

4. The water _____ was beautiful.   bend   pack   fall

5. When she yells, I be _____ angry.   look   come   want

6. _____ times I eat ice cream.   Be   Some   House

☞ **Feedback** In two, hook *rain* to the front of *drops* and you have *raindrops*, one word made of two little words. In three, *jelly + beans* makes the word *jellybeans*. In four, *water + fall = waterfall*. In five, *be + come = become*. In six, *Some + times = Sometimes*.

Now learn to spot **word endings**. You add **endings** to many words when you use them in different ways.

End is a word. You add <u>ing</u> to **end** to make **end<u>ing</u>**.
You add <u>ed</u> to **add** to make **add<u>ed</u>**.

And <u>es</u> added to **go** makes **go<u>es</u>**.

You can add <u>s</u> to words when you mean many.
Add <u>s</u> to **book** to make **book<u>s</u>**.

Task 2 Read the sentences and then circle the word **ending** in the word that best completes each sentence. The first is done for you.

1. Sadie _____ her soda slowly.   drink(s)   drinking

2. Jim _____ a big fish.   hooked   hooking

3. Tom _____ his car on Tuesdays.   washing   washes

4. It was _____ when I woke up.   rained   raining

5. My bird _____ when he sees me.   laughs   laughing

6. I saw many _____ last week.   movied   movies

☞ **Feedback** In two, the correct word ending is *ed* in *hooked*. In three, *es* is added to *wash* to make *washes*. In four, *ing* is the ending in *raining*. In five, *s* is added to *laugh*, and in six, *s* is added to *movie*.

When **affixes** or **word parts** are added to words, the meanings of the words change. One kind of affix is called a **prefix**. **Pre-** is a **prefix** that means *before*. When you add the prefix **pre-** to the word **fix**, it means that you fix, or add, something to the <u>beginning</u> of a word. The word **preschool** means *before going to regular school*.

Task 3 These prefixes mean *not:* **dis-**, **un-**, **il-**. Write what each word means. The first is done for you.

1. The prefix **un-** means *not*. An <u>**un**laced</u> shoe is *not laced*.

   Unhappy means <u>not happy</u>.

   Unkind means _____.

2. The prefix **dis-** means *not*. To <u>**dis**agree</u> is to *not agree*.

   Dislike means _____.

   Distrust means _____.

3. The prefix **im-** means *not*. **Impossible** means *not possible*.

Improper means _____.

Impolite means _____.

4. The prefix **il-** means *not*. To be **illegal** is to *not be legal*.

Illiterate means _____.

Illogical means _____.

☞ **Feedback** If **un-**, **dis-**, **im-**, and **il-** mean *not*, then **unkind** means *not kind*. In two, **dislike** and **distrust** mean to *not like* and to *not trust*. **Improper** means *not proper*, and **impolite** means *not polite*. An **illiterate** is *not literate*, *cannot read*. And **illogical** is *not logical*.

Task 4

Here are two more prefixes: **mis-**, **re-**. Write what each word means.

1. The prefix **mis-** means *wrong* or *badly*. To **misread** is to *read badly*.

To **misspell** means _____

_____.

To **misplace** something means _____

_____.

2. The prefix **re-** means *again*. To **rewrite** is to *write something again*.

To **retell** means _____

_____.

To **retrace** your steps means to _____

_____.

☞ **Feedback** To **misspell** is to *spell a word wrong or incorrectly*. To **misplace** is to *put in a wrong place so that you can't find it*. In two, to **retell** is to *tell again*. To **retrace** is to *trace again or go over something again*.

Here are three more prefixes: **trans-**, **inter-**, **sub-**. Write what each word means.

1. The prefix **trans-** means *across* or *beyond*. One meaning of the word **port** is to *carry*. So to **transport** is to *carry across or beyond*.

   If you have a **transatlantic** phone call, you are talking to someone

   _____.

2. The prefix **inter-** means *between* or *among*. **International** means *between* or *among nations*.

   Intercollegiate events are events _____

   _____.

3. The prefix **sub-** means *under*. A **submarine** goes *under the water*.

   Subsoil means _____.

☞ **Feedback** In one, **transatlantic** telephone calls go *across the Atlantic Ocean*. **Intercollegiate** events are events *between colleges*. *Soil that is just under the surface is* **subsoil**.

You can be a word detective without knowing these underlined words. Using the prefix as a clue, a word detective can make a good guess. Circle the letter of your guess.

1. Her hair was <u>unkempt</u>.

   A neat   C wet

   B not neat   D dry

2. He <u>misappropriated</u> the money.

   A used it badly   C carried it

   B spent it before   D went back

☞ **Feedback** In one, in the word *unkempt*, **un-** means *not*. So B, *not neat*, is your best guess. In two, **mis-** means *badly*, so you can guess that A is the right answer. You don't have to know the word. Use the prefix to make a good guess.

3. She <u>subverted</u> the system.

    A carried it over   C snuck under

    B did it first   D ended

4. He <u>disengaged</u> the gear.

    A hung it   C made it not work

    B put it under   D put it between

☞ **Feedback** Remember, spot the prefix and use it as a clue. The answer to three is C, because **sub-** means *under*. Four is C, because **dis-** means *not*.

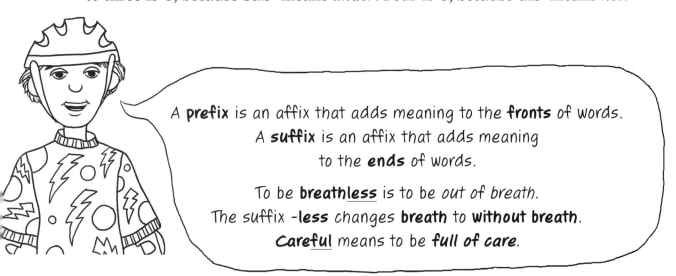

A **prefix** is an affix that adds meaning to the **fronts** of words.
A **suffix** is an affix that adds meaning
to the **ends** of words.

To be **breath<u>less</u>** is to be *out of breath*.
The suffix -**less** changes **breath** to **without breath**.
Care<u>ful</u> means to be **full of care**.

Task 7

Here are three suffixes: **-ful**, **-less**, **-ous**. Write what each word means. The first is done for you.

1. The suffix **-ful** means *full of*. **Truth<u>ful</u>** means *full of truth*.

    Thankful means _____ full of thanks _____.

2. The suffix **-less** means to *be without*. **Thank<u>less</u>** means *without thanks*.

    Careless means _____.

3. The suffix **-ous** means *full of,* or *lots of*, or *full*. **Danger<u>ous</u>** means *full of danger*.

    Famous means _____.

☞ **Feedback** In two, **care<u>less</u>** means to *be without care*. In three, a **fam<u>ous</u>** person has *lots of fame*.

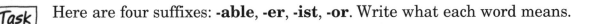

Task 8

Here are four suffixes: **-able**, **-er**, **-ist**, **-or**. Write what each word means.

1. The suffix **-able** means *able*. Sometimes it is spelled **-ible**. She is **love<u>able</u>**. Loveable means *able to be loved*.

   This job is doable. **Doable** means _____.

2. The suffixes **-er** and **-ist** mean *someone who does something*. A **paint<u>er</u>** paints. A **humor<u>ist</u>** is *someone who makes you laugh*. Sometimes the **-er** suffix is spelled **-or**, as in **sail<u>or</u>**.

   A **balloon<u>ist</u>** is someone who _____.

    ☞ **Feedback** In one, **doable** is *able to do*. In two, a **balloonist** is someone who *flies balloons*.

Task 9

Remember, you don't have to know the meaning of a word. Try to guess the meaning from the suffix. Circle your guess.

1. A <u>palpable</u> lie is one that people are _____
   A friendly.   B very long.   C able to detect.

2. A <u>procurer</u> of cars is _____
   A someone who buys.   B a large supply.   C a place to hide.

3. To be <u>guiltless</u> is to _____
   A be very clever.   B have no guilt.   C have lots of money.

   ☞ **Feedback** One is C, *able*. Two is A, *someone*. Three is B, *no*.

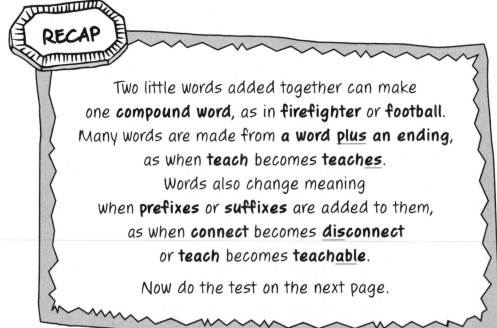

RECAP

Two little words added together can make
one **compound word**, as in **firefighter** or **football**.
Many words are made from **a word <u>plus</u> an ending**,
as when **teach** becomes **teach<u>es</u>**.
Words also change meaning
when **prefixes** or **suffixes** are added to them,
as when **connect** becomes **disconnect**
or **teach** becomes **teach<u>able</u>**.

Now do the test on the next page.

See how much you've learned. Take this test.

Questions 1–6. Read the key word. Choose the word or phrase that gives the best meaning of the underlined prefix or suffix. Fill in the circle beside the answer you choose.

1. meaning<u>less</u>
   - Ⓐ without
   - Ⓑ of or like
   - Ⓒ able to be
   - Ⓓ lots of

2. <u>pre</u>planned
   - Ⓐ after
   - Ⓑ before
   - Ⓒ able to
   - Ⓓ across

3. <u>dis</u>entangle
   - Ⓐ able to
   - Ⓑ into
   - Ⓒ under
   - Ⓓ not

4. <u>re</u>live
   - Ⓐ go away
   - Ⓑ not
   - Ⓒ a person
   - Ⓓ again

5. <u>un</u>noticed
   - Ⓐ not
   - Ⓑ see
   - Ⓒ badly
   - Ⓓ after

6. ment<u>or</u>
   - Ⓐ without
   - Ⓑ of or like
   - Ⓒ after
   - Ⓓ person who

Questions 7–9. Read each incomplete sentence. Choose the correct meaning of the underlined word. Fill in the circle beside the answer you choose.

7. To be <u>uninhabited</u> means to _____
   - Ⓐ be far away.
   - Ⓑ be very happy.
   - Ⓒ have no inhabitants.
   - Ⓓ like lots of people.

8. To <u>intercede</u> in two people's activities is to _____
   - Ⓐ laugh at them.
   - Ⓑ get between them.
   - Ⓒ pick a fight with them.
   - Ⓓ ignore them.

9. To <u>subjugate</u> yourself to someone's authority is to _____
   - Ⓐ put yourself under it.
   - Ⓑ get far away from it.
   - Ⓒ listen to what others say.
   - Ⓓ make up your own mind.

Questions 10–12. Look at the key word. Find the word that can be added to the key word to make a compound word. Fill in the circle beside the answer you choose.

10. grape
    - Ⓐ shoe
    - Ⓑ gum
    - Ⓒ vine
    - Ⓓ money

11. summer
    - Ⓐ paper
    - Ⓑ time
    - Ⓒ days
    - Ⓓ plant

12. coat
    - Ⓐ over
    - Ⓑ winter
    - Ⓒ sweater
    - Ⓓ new

STOP

Number Correct/Total=_____ /12

3 Word Meaning

Identifying the meaning of words

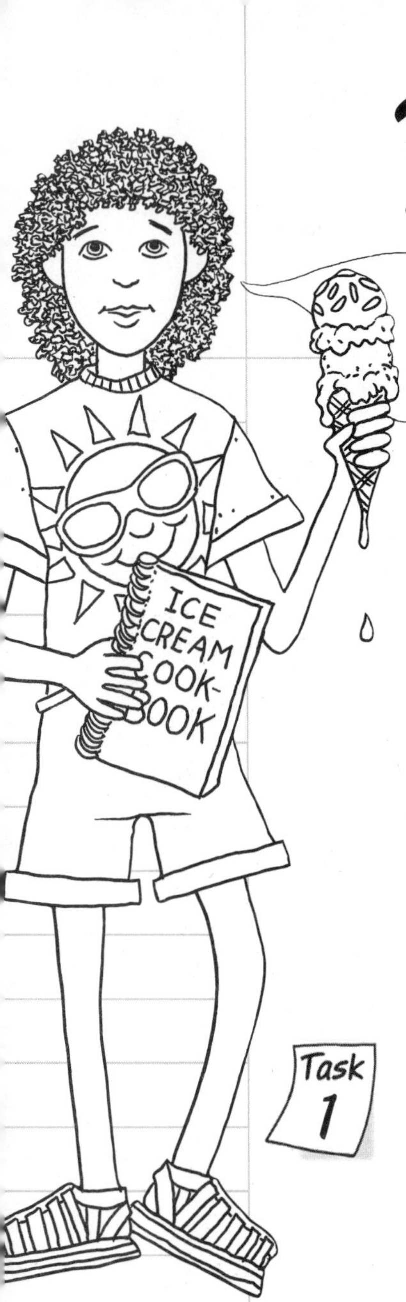

> On the next two pages you will **learn words** you need to know to read some of the stories in this book.

height	Giraffes grow to great **heights**. Long necks make giraffes very tall.
weigh	Because of their *height*, giraffes are heavy. They **weigh** a lot.
factory	A **factory** manufactures scales. Scales are used to *weigh* giraffes.
tongue	A whale's **tongue** *weighs* a lot.
nostrils	You breathe through your **nostrils**. **Nostrils** are holes in your nose.

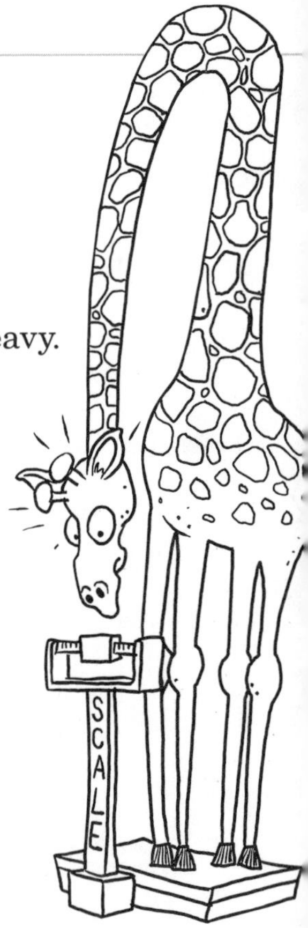

Task 1

Write your answers to these questions.

1. What is your weight? How much do you weigh?

   _____

2. What is your height? How tall are you?

   _____

3. Stick out your tongue. How long is it?

   _____

4. Are your nostrils above or below your tongue?

   _____

5. What is a building where scales are made called?

   _____

☞ **Feedback** Do you remember your **weight** and **height**? How long do you think your **tongue** is? I hope your **nostrils** aren't below your **tongue**! Of course, **scales** are made in a **factory**.

More New Words To Use

roasted   Do you **roast** chicken in an oven?
I'm **roasting** in this heat!

potato   I like *roasted* **potatoes**.
I dug **potatoes** out of the ground.

swallow   Don't **swallow** a hot *potato*. Cool it first.

nibble   If a *potato* is hot, **nibble** it. Take little bites.
Don't *swallow* it whole.

sniff   Do you **sniff** your food before you *swallow*?

Task 2   Read this story. Then circle the letters of the answers.

> At first, Nelson sniffed the food. But he had the sniffles and couldn't smell much. So he nibbled at the roasted potatoes. They were too hot to swallow.
>
> "I must not eat all the potatoes," he said. "The people have to eat too. I'll just make a little sandwich. I'll put some potatoes in between two slices of bread and make a potato sandwich."
>
> Have you ever seen a rabbit eat a sandwich? He nibbles and nibbles for a very long time. Poor Nelson took a whole hour just to eat one sandwich. It was enough to put weight on his tiny belly.
>
> "Now I weigh enough to play rabbit football," he said. "And if I grow more, I'll have the height to play rabbit basketball too."

1. Why can't Nelson smell food?

   A   It is too hot.   C   He has the sniffles.

   B   He has no nostrils.   D   He swallows fast.

2. How does Nelson eat the potatoes?

   A   He gulps them down.   C   He roasts them.

   B   He licks them.   D   He nibbles them.

3. How long does it take Nelson to eat the potato sandwich?

   A   an hour   C   a week

   B   a day   D   a year

☞ **Feedback** In one, Nelson has a cold. His *sniffles* get in the way of his sniffing. Like most rabbits, Nelson *nibbles* his food. It takes him *an hour* to eat his potato sandwich. What a strange meal!

When endings are added to words, the words look different. You might miss simple words because the endings fool you.

Words can be **sneaky**. **Sneaky** is **sneak** with a **y** at the end. The words **dragged**, **sagged**, and **bragged** are from the simple words **drag**, **sag**, and **brag**. Today I **brag** about my A in spelling. Yesterday I **bragged** about it too.

Task 3 Fill in the missing word.

1. **argue** To *argue* means to *fight with words*, to *disagree*. I **argued** with her. We had an **argument** yesterday.

   We were _____ over a cookie.

    Feedback The word *argue* becomes *arguing*.

2. **spy** To *spy* is to *catch sight of something*, to *see it closely*. **Spying** the bluejay in the tree is hard.

   Yesterday I _____ a bird.

3. **fascinate** To *fascinate* means to *interest*. The story about Columbus **fascinated** me.

   The way rabbits nibble food is _____.

4. **solve** To *solve* is to *work out a problem*.

   When you **solve** a problem, you have a **solution** or a **resolution**. It's your **solution** to the problem. We **solved** the problem of the hot potato by cooling it.

   We were _____ a math problem when you called.

5. **peace** To be at *peace* is to *be calm*.

   Without war, we are **peaceful**. We **peacefully** solved the problem.

   All is _____ now that we have **peace**.

    Feedback In two, I *spied*. In three, the way rabbits nibble food can be *fascinating*, and in four, we were *solving* a problem. The answer to five is *peaceful*.

How many different ways can people speak?
They can **whisper, chatter, yell, cry, scream, call, babble, gossip, shout, cheer, declare, proclaim, roar, screech, howl, shriek, squeal,** and **speak** in many more ways.

Do you know all these words?
If not, use your dictionary to do Task Four.

Task 4

Circle the best word that describes what sound the person or animal probably makes.

1. A wolf _____

   whispers.   squeals.   howls.   chatters.

2. Monkeys _____

   roared.   yelled.   whispered.   chattered.

3. When I tickled her, she _____, "Stop! Ha, ha! Stop!"

   babbled   declared   proclaimed   squealed

4. When I jumped from behind the plant, she was so frightened that she _____

   shrieked.   called.   cheered.   whispered.

5. "Get out of here! Get out of here, now!" he _____ in anger.

   babbled   roared   proclaimed   whispered

6. When people tell stories about other people, we say they are _____

   declaring.   gossiping.   proclaiming.   yelling.

7. If I call to you from across the field, then I must _____

   cry.   shout.   whisper.   declare.

8. A formal way to speak is to _____

   yell.   babble.   gossip.   proclaim.

☞ **Feedback** In one, a wolf *howls*. Monkeys *chattered* in two. In three, she *squealed* when tickled. Do you *squeal* or *shriek* when you're tickled? In four, she *shrieked*, and in five, he *roared*. *Gossiping* is telling stories about other people that may or may not be true. Are you a gossip? In seven, you must *shout* across a field, and eight is *proclaim*.

How many different ways can people see things?
They can **peer, peek, gaze, spot, glance, stare,
observe, notice, behold, view,** and **see** in many other ways.

If you need to, use your dictionary to do Task Five.

GRAND CAN

Task 5 Circle the <u>best</u> word to describe how the person or animal uses its eyes.

1. When I entered the room I _____ her hiding behind the piano.

   peered   glanced   noticed   stared

2. To look quickly or briefly is to _____

   notice.   observe.   view.   glance.

3. When you see the Grand Canyon, you _____ one of the great sights in nature.

   spy   behold   peeked at   spot

4. We _____ the people walking in the street on Easter Sunday.

   peered   stared   observed   glanced

5. To glance quickly is to _____

   peer.   view.   peek.   stare.

👉 **Feedback** In one, I *noticed* her hiding. In two, a brief look is to *glance*, but in three, you don't want a **peek** at a great sight in nature. Instead, you want to *behold* it. In four, we *observed*, and in five, another word for **glance** or **quick look** is *peek*.

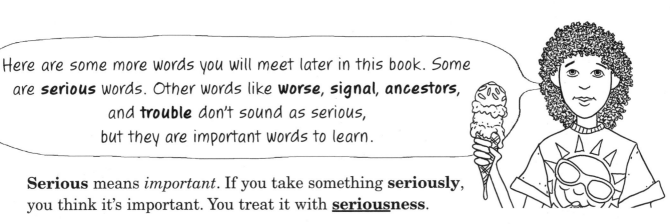

Here are some more words you will meet later in this book. Some are **serious** words. Other words like **worse**, **signal**, **ancestors**, and **trouble** don't sound as serious, but they are important words to learn.

Serious means *important*. If you take something **seriously**, you think it's important. You treat it with **<u>seriousness</u>**.

Trouble means *there's a problem*. And that's bad. **Serious trouble** is even worse than bad trouble!

"You're in serious trouble, young man."

Your **ancestors** are *the people who came before you*. Your grandma is one of your **ancestors**.

Task 6

Circle the <u>best</u> word to complete the sentence.

1. Something important is _____
   A solved.
   B serious.
   C measured.
   D worse.

2. My great-grandfather was my first _____ to come to America.
   A problem
   B spot
   C notice
   D ancestor

3. To announce something in a very formal way is to _____
   A behold.
   B proclaim.
   C observe.
   D argue.

4. To get someone's weight or height, you _____
   A resolve.
   B gossip.
   C measure.
   D swallow.

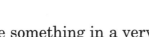 **Feedback** The answers are: one—B, two—D, three—B, four—C.

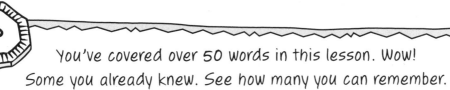

RECAP

You've covered over 50 words in this lesson. Wow! Some you already knew. See how many you can remember. Do the test on the next page.

See how much you've learned. Take this test.

1. A <u>problem</u> usually means there is _____
   - Ⓐ serious.
   - Ⓑ declaration.
   - Ⓒ trouble.
   - Ⓓ argument.

2. Another word for <u>observe</u> is _____
   - Ⓐ manufacture.
   - Ⓑ gossip.
   - Ⓒ argue.
   - Ⓓ behold.

3. My <u>aunt's mother's mother</u> is one of my _____
   - Ⓐ parents.
   - Ⓑ ancestors.
   - Ⓒ observations.
   - Ⓓ fascinations.

4. A <u>place that manufactures</u> is called a _____
   - Ⓐ height.
   - Ⓑ factory.
   - Ⓒ swallow.
   - Ⓓ peek.

5. To <u>resolve</u> a problem is to _____
   - Ⓐ declare it.
   - Ⓑ argue it.
   - Ⓒ solve it.
   - Ⓓ notice it.

6. To <u>look</u> with interest and pleasure is to _____
   - Ⓐ gaze.
   - Ⓑ whisper.
   - Ⓒ weigh.
   - Ⓓ measure.

7. When two people <u>argue</u>, they _____
   - Ⓐ observe.
   - Ⓑ notices.
   - Ⓒ resolve.
   - Ⓓ disagree.

8. To announce or <u>declare</u> in a formal way is to _____
   - Ⓐ solve.
   - Ⓑ proclaim.
   - Ⓒ fascinate.
   - Ⓓ notice.

9. To <u>speak</u> very softly is to _____
   - Ⓐ whisper.
   - Ⓑ shriek.
   - Ⓒ declare.
   - Ⓓ resolve.

10. A <u>measure of how tall</u> you are is called _____
    - Ⓐ weight.
    - Ⓑ declaration.
    - Ⓒ solution.
    - Ⓓ height.

11. The <u>part of your mouth</u> that helps you taste and swallow is your _____
    - Ⓐ tongue.
    - Ⓑ nostril.
    - Ⓒ serious.
    - Ⓓ resolution.

12. <u>Ancestors</u> are _____
    - Ⓐ parents.
    - Ⓑ people.
    - Ⓒ great-grandparents.
    - Ⓓ fascinates.

STOP

Number Correct/Total=_____ /12

4 Synonyms and Antonyms

Understanding words that mean the same and words that mean the opposite

A word that means the same,
or nearly the same, as another word
is called a **synonym**.

Synonyms are **easy**. They are **simple** to learn.

Task 1

Shall we take a **walk**? Do you want to take a **stroll**? These two questions mean the same thing. **Stroll** and **walk** are **synonyms**. Circle the synonym for each underlined word.

1. together	apart	united
2. shy	sleepy	bashful
3. recall	remember	amuse
4. eating	inciting	devouring
5. odd	add	strange
6. finish	complete	starry
7. funny	serious	amusing
8. laughable	amusing	serious

☞ **Feedback** The synonyms are: *together* and *united*, *shy* and *bashful*, *recall* and *remember*, *eating* and *devouring*, *odd* and *strange*, *finish* and *complete*, *funny* and *amusing*, *laughable* and *amusing*.

Task 2

Some of these word pairs are synonyms. Some are not.
If they mean the same, or about the same, circle the pair.

1. above	overhead	4. previous	after
2. wrong	incorrect	5. inside	incite
3. declare	proclaim	6. poke	punch

☞ **Feedback** Numbers 1, 2, 3, and 6 are synonyms.
The other two are not.

Remember, **almost the same** is good enough for you to call two words *synonyms*.

Task 3 Circle the <u>best</u> synonym for each underlined word. Be careful. More than one answer could fit, but only one <u>best</u> fits as the synonym for the underlined word.

1. <u>gather</u> flowers   plant   collect   enjoy

2. <u>conceal</u> the answer   protect   save   hide

3. flowers grow in <u>swamps</u>   gardens   ponds   oceans

4. <u>swamped</u> with phone calls   wet   overloaded   painted

5. <u>drowned</u> in phone calls   wet   soaked   swamped

 Feedback In one, someone who wants to enjoy flowers might *gather* or *collect* them. *Collect* fits best as the synonym for **gather**. In two, to **conceal** is to *hide*. You may *hide* or *conceal* things to protect them, but *protect* doesn't mean the same as *conceal*, so *hide* is the best fit. In three, **swamps** and *ponds* are synonyms. But in four, to be **swamped** with telephone calls is to be *overloaded*, not wet. And five says the same thing, but it uses *swamped* as the synonym for **drowned**. If you're *drowned* or *swamped* with calls, you're *overloaded*. Nobody got wet, but the writer wants you to think of phone calls pouring in like water. That's why *swamped* is the synonym and *wet* isn't. Synonyms like these make stories even more fun to read.

6. <u>frightened</u> by the noise   angry   uncomfortable   terrified

7. a <u>terrific</u> meal   great   terrified   long

8. <u>timid</u> about speaking   joyful   terrified   fearful

9. <u>performed</u> his tasks   did   acted   played

10. <u>purchased</u> something   owned   carried   bought

☞ **Feedback** In six, *frightened*, *angry*, and *terrified* are all *uncomfortable* feelings. But *terrified* is the synonym for **frightened**. In seven, **terrific** looks like *terrified*, but the word *terrific* means something *great* or *special*. In eight, **timid** means *a little bit afraid*, which is why *fearful*, not *terrified*, is the right answer. In nine, **perform a task** is to *do a task*, as in "He *did* his tasks." In ten, she *bought* something is the answer.

Task 4 Here are nine synonyms you can use instead of the underlined words in this story. First, draw a line through each <u>underlined word</u> in the story. Then on the line, write the number of the synonym you chose to take its place. Two are done for you. You do the rest.

Use these synonyms.

1. funny
2. project
3. buddy
4. explanation
5. created
6. sculpture
7. bothered
8. favored
9. destroying

She didn't give me a good ~~reason~~ _4_ for smashing ____

the statue. All she said was, "I didn't like it. It ~~annoyed~~ _7_

me to see the <u>statue</u> ____ sitting out there all alone."

She <u>preferred</u> ____ putting another statue next to it. She

thought the statue needed a <u>companion</u> ____ to keep it

company. She laughed, but I didn't think it was so <u>comical</u> ____.

After all, I was the one who <u>made</u> ____ the statue, and it was

not an easy <u>job</u> ____ to complete.

☞ **Feedback** If you wrote in the synonym numbers in this order, 4, 9, 7, 6, 8, 3, 1, 5, 2, the story will read like this.

She didn't give me a good <u>explanation</u> for <u>destroying</u> the statue. All she said was, "I didn't like it. It <u>bothered</u> me to see the <u>sculpture</u> sitting out there all alone."

She <u>favored</u> putting another statue next to it. She thought the statue needed a <u>buddy</u> to keep it company. She laughed, but I didn't think it was so <u>funny</u>. After all, I was the one who <u>created</u> the statue, and it was not an easy <u>project</u> to complete.

A word that means the opposite, or nearly the opposite, of another word is called an **antonym**.

Antonyms are **easy**. They're not **difficult** to learn.

Task 5

This time look for antonyms, not synonyms. For example, *committee* and *group* are synonyms, but *group* and *individual* are **antonyms**. Like *fat* and *thin*, they're **opposites**. Circle the best antonym for each numbered word.

1. quick	quiet	fast	slow
2. disappear	appear	caring	speeding
3. stare	stair	move	glance
4. energetic	tried	wheel	weary
5. upset	frantic	calm	final
6. war	peace	struggle	game

☞ **Feedback** In one, *quick* and *slow* are antonyms, followed by *disappear / appear* in two. A *stare* is a long, slow look while a *glance* is the opposite. In four, even if you don't know the word *energetic*, it's close enough to *energy* for you to guess it's an antonym to *weary*, which means *tired*. The other antonyms, or opposites, are *upset* and *calm* and *war and peace*.

Task 6

Write an antonym for each word.

1. light _____   4. stand _____

2. wet _____   5. loud _____

3. good _____   6. early _____

☞ **Feedback** Some antonyms you could use are *light / dark*, *wet / dry*, *good / bad*, *stand / sit*, *loud / soft*, *early / late*.

When you exchanged words for their synonyms in Task Four, the words changed but the story stayed the same. What happens if you change words to their opposite meanings, to **antonyms**? Some funny things can happen. Try it in Task Seven.

Task 7

Use all nine antonyms in this list to replace the underlined words in this letter. First, draw a line through each underlined word in the letter. Then on the line, write the number of the antonym you chose to take its place. Two are done for you. You do the rest.

Use these antonyms.

1. day
2. summer
3. fast
4. uncomfortable
5. ceiling
6. can
7. few
8. warm
9. doesn't

Dear Jim,

I ~~can't~~ **6** see why you built your house so slowly ____ . It ~~does~~ **9** have a floor ____ . Aren't you cold ____ in the winter ____ during the night ____ ?

I don't think I'd be comfortable ____ living there. But most ____ other people would like it.

Best wishes,
Jerry

☞ **Feedback** After you put in the antonyms for the underlined words, the letter reads like this.

Dear Jim,

I <u>can</u> see why you built your house so <u>fast</u>. It <u>doesn't</u> have a <u>ceiling</u>. Aren't you <u>warm</u> in the <u>summer</u> during the <u>day</u>? I don't think I'd be <u>uncomfortable</u> living there. But <u>few</u> other people would like it.

Best wishes,
Jerry

Here are some words you will read later in this book. For each numbered word, write **S** over the Synonym and **A** over the Antonym. Leave all others blank. The first one is done for you.

1. beautiful · careful · _A_ ugly · soft · _S_ pretty · amuse
2. mournful · night · grieving · happy · tardy
3. sturdy · weak · loud · large · strong
4. dragged · pushed · spoke · pulled · hurt
5. peaceful · friendly · calm · warlike · tricky
6. fascinating · dull · sharp · interesting · tall
7. before · in front of · aside · after · near
8. amuse · bore · entertain · sing · count
9. closer · below · nearer · above · farther
10. less · some · most · more · fewer
11. danger · fear · safety · peril · hurt
12. known · familiar · strange · learn · heard

👉 **Feedback** When someone dies you **mourn**. So in two, *grieving* is the synonym and *happy* is the antonym. **Sturdy** means *strong*, so *weak* is the opposite. In four, you **drag** or *pull* things, the opposite of *pushing* them. In five, **peaceful** is *calm*; *warlike* is the antonym. In six, **fascinating** is *interesting*, the opposite of *dull*. In seven, *in front of*, although it is a phrase, not a word, is the synonym for **before**; *after* is the antonym. In eight, **amusing** people *entertain*; the antonym is *bore*. In nine, *farther* is the antonym for **closer**, and its synonym is *nearer*. In ten and eleven, **less** is *fewer*, not *more*, and **danger** is *peril*, not *safety*. In twelve, a **known** word is *familiar*; the antonym is *strange*.

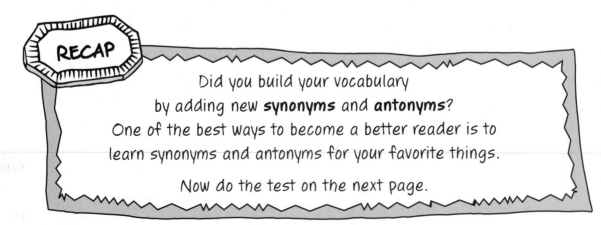

RECAP

Did you build your vocabulary by adding new **synonyms** and **antonyms**? One of the best ways to become a better reader is to learn synonyms and antonyms for your favorite things.

Now do the test on the next page.

See how much you've learned. Take this test.

Questions 1–5. Find the word that means the same, or almost the same, as the underlined word. Fill in the circle beside the word you choose.

1. the <u>fixed</u> watch
   - Ⓐ replied
   - Ⓑ registered
   - Ⓒ remade
   - Ⓓ repaired

2. very <u>bashful</u>
   - Ⓐ bright
   - Ⓑ tired
   - Ⓒ shy
   - Ⓓ red

3. kept <u>scaring</u>
   - Ⓐ hurting
   - Ⓑ terrifying
   - Ⓒ marking
   - Ⓓ crying

4. <u>dragged</u> it
   - Ⓐ pushed
   - Ⓑ pulled
   - Ⓒ grabbed
   - Ⓓ hurled

5. <u>build</u> a school
   - Ⓐ construct
   - Ⓑ conduct
   - Ⓒ convert
   - Ⓓ concert

Questions 6–10. Find the word that means the opposite of the underlined word. Fill in the circle beside the answer you choose.

6. was <u>tardy</u>
   - Ⓐ neat
   - Ⓑ early
   - Ⓒ late
   - Ⓓ small

7. very <u>rude</u>
   - Ⓐ unfriendly
   - Ⓑ young
   - Ⓒ angry
   - Ⓓ polite

8. an <u>increase</u>
   - Ⓐ more
   - Ⓑ lessening
   - Ⓒ opening
   - Ⓓ mistake

9. is <u>mistaken</u>
   - Ⓐ in error
   - Ⓑ right
   - Ⓒ answered
   - Ⓓ incorrect

10. was <u>weird</u>
    - Ⓐ normal
    - Ⓑ strange
    - Ⓒ unusual
    - Ⓓ huge

STOP

Number Correct/Total=_____ /10

5 Sentence Clues

Using sentence clues to get meaning

You can guess what the next word will be in a sentence even before you see it! The sentence gives you **clues**. Try this:

She fell into the water and got all w____.

You can guess the missing word, because the rest of the sentence gives you a *context*. **Context is the meaning you get from all the other words**.

Task 1 Guess the missing words. Write your answers.

1. Sergio dipped his dirty hands into the w __ __ __ __ and washed them.

2. The mother bird fed her three b __ __ __ birds.

3. In the summer it gets very h __ __, but in the winter it snows.

☞ **Feedback** You can guess that Sergio washed his dirty hands in *water*. The mother bird must have fed her *baby* birds. In winter it's cold, but in summer it's *hot*.

Task 2 In the next story, some words are left out. Choose and circle the word that best fits each numbered missing word in the story. Number one is done for you.

Long ago, so long ago that the sky had no stars but always had a full __1__, there lived an old lady named Lucy. The lady was a hundred years __2__. On her birthday, she went to the town hall for her big birthday __3__.

1. noon   (moon)   sun

2. cold   all   old

3. pantry   party   pretty

The king came because he wanted to see someone who had lived a __4__ years. He gave her a birthday __5__ of many diamonds.

On her way home, the moon went behind some __6__. Without the moon, the night got very __7__. So the old lady threw the diamonds into the sky and made the __8__.

4. hunting   hundred   haunted   7. dark   draw   dawn

5. present   pretty   prepare   8. houses   trees   stars

6. stars   crowds   clouds

☞ **Feedback** For two, the missing word has to be *old*. The words *cold* and *all* don't make sense in that sentence context. And three must be *party*. You can tell from the context that four is *hundred*, and five must be *present*. *Clouds* is the best guess for six. And in this context, *dark* is the choice for seven. For eight, that is one myth about how the *stars* were born. See how guessing at words in context can help you read better?

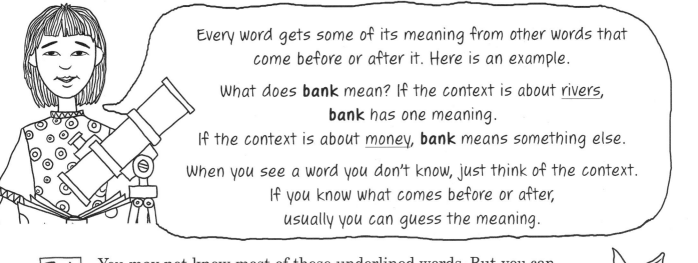

Every word gets some of its meaning from other words that come before or after it. Here is an example.

What does **bank** mean? If the context is about <u>rivers</u>, **bank** has one meaning.
If the context is about <u>money</u>, **bank** means something else.

When you see a word you don't know, just think of the context. If you know what comes before or after, usually you can guess the meaning.

Task 3

You may not know most of these underlined words. But you can guess from **context** what they mean. Circle the answer.

1. The dog snarled, growled, and came closer. It looked <u>vicious</u>.
   Vicious probably means the dog would _____
   bite.   laugh.   sleep.   cry.

2. Most dogs are gentle. They lick your hand and are very <u>gregarious</u>.
   Gregarious probably means _____
   vicious.   terrified.   friendly.   crazy.

GRRRR!

☞ **Feedback** In one, a snarling, growling dog could *bite*. It looks **vicious**. In two, a gentle dog is *friendly* or **gregarious**.

Task
4

You've probaby never seen most of these underlined words. Now that you know how to use the context, you can make good guesses about what each means. Circle your answers.

1. Carol dropped Peter's ice cream, and he began to cry. What a sad and <u>doleful</u> look he had on his face.

   Doleful means _____

   A unhappy.   C cheerful.

   B happy.   D calm.

2. The balloon popped when she <u>punctured</u> it.

   To *puncture* means to _____

   A paint.   C put a hole in it.

   B melt.   D let it sail away.

3. Carefully he crept to the <u>brink</u> of the hole and looked down into the deep well.

   Brink means _____

   A bottom.   C fence.

   B large.   D edge.

☞ **Feedback** For one, in the context of crying and sad, **doleful** must be A, *unhappy*. In two, a balloon popping is the context for C, *put a hole in it*. In three, the context of looking down the hole puts him at the *edge*, D. Do you see how context helps you guess words you may never have seen before?

4. His mouth was so sore he could hardly chew. So he <u>nibbled</u> his food.

   Nibble means _____

   A to take big gulps.   C gobble slowly.

   B to take tiny bites.   D drink slowly.

5. The race car blew a tire, went out of control, and <u>careened</u> off the wall.

 To *careen* means to _____

 A fly. C bounce.

 B jump. D speed.

6. They finished the house and poured the <u>cement</u> for the driveway.

 Cement is what _____ are made of.

 A airplanes C roofs

 B cars D sidewalks

☞ **Feedback** In four, **nibble** is to *take tiny bites*, B. In five, the context of a race car out of control is the clue that **careened** means to *bounce*. In six, *sidewalks*, D, is right.

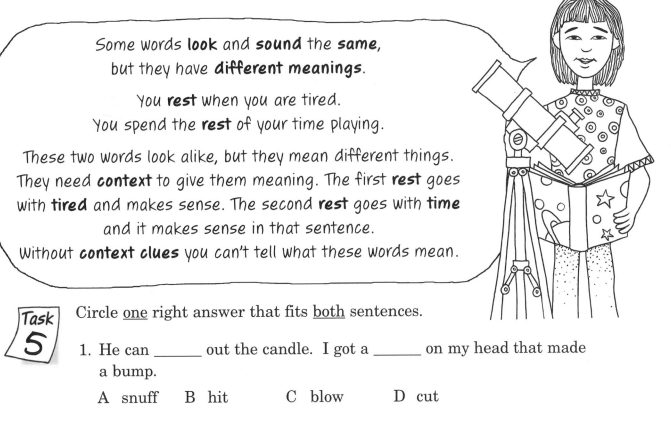

Some words **look** and **sound** the **same**, but they have **different meanings**.

You **rest** when you are tired.
You spend the **rest** of your time playing.

These two words look alike, but they mean different things. They need **context** to give them meaning. The first **rest** goes with **tired** and makes sense. The second **rest** goes with **time** and it makes sense in that sentence.
Without **context clues** you can't tell what these words mean.

Task 5

Circle <u>one</u> right answer that fits <u>both</u> sentences.

1. He can _____ out the candle. I got a _____ on my head that made a bump.

 A snuff   B hit   C blow   D cut

2. The children liked to play _____. Her clothes had a price _____.

 A ball   B tag   C apples   D take

3. She needed to water the _____. She worked at the local _____.

 A grass   B school   C flowers   D plant

☞ **Feedback** In one, *blow* fits both sentences. In two, *tag* is the correct word with two different meanings. In three, D, *plant*, is right.

Task 6

This time you must get the context and then write what the word is.

1. This word means *a container of soup*. It also means you're *able to do something*. It has only three letters and begins with **c**.

   The word is _____.

2. This word means *all the actors in a movie* and also *what you do with a fishing rod*. It can also be *something doctors put on your broken leg*.

   The word is _____.

3. This word means a *a piece of metal that screws on a bolt* and it also means *something you eat*.

   The word is _____.

☞ **Feedback** In one, these two different contexts <u>can</u> work with *can*. You *can* buy soup in a *can*, can you not? In two, all the actors in a movie are the *cast*, you *cast* a fishing rod, and you wear a *cast* on a broken leg. In three, a *nut* screws onto a bolt and is also a food.

Task 7

Here are some words you'll need to know to read stories later in this book. If you don't know a word, use context clues to guess. Be sure to read <u>all</u> the clues. More than one word may fit the sentence. Circle the one that fits <u>best</u>.

1. They measured how tall it is and its _____
   Which word means *how heavy something is*?
   A height.   B weight.   C width.   D length.

2. They measured how heavy she is and her _____
   Which word means *how tall someone is*?
   A height.   B weight.   C width.   D length.

3. They put Carlos on a scale to _____ him.
   Which word means to find *Carlos's weight*?
   A measure   B weigh   C read   D guess

☞ **Feedback** In one, they measured *weight*. In two, *height* tells how tall someone is. In three, scales are used to find out how much Carlos *weighs*—no *t* in this word.

Task 8

Many American words come from Native American words and from other countries. The Old English word **lytel** gave us our modern word *little*. Task Eight gives you old words from these languages. Can you guess the modern words used today? Circle the letter of the best correct answer.

1. Some Native Americans ate meat and a *batata*.

   Today *batata* is also known as a _____

   A potato.   B bagel.   C popcorn.   D fish.

2. In Old England they cut a *slitte* for a buttonhole.

   Today we have the word _____

   A slab.   B slow.   C plate.   D slit.

3. In Old English a man might bite his *tunge*.

   Today he tries not to bite his _____

   A teeth.   B tongue.   C lips.   D cheeks.

☞ **Feedback** In one, if you say **batata**, it sounds like *potato*. A is the right answer. In two, a buttonhole looks like a *slit*, which is close to **slitte**. In three, you can guess that speakers of Old English bit their *tongues* too.

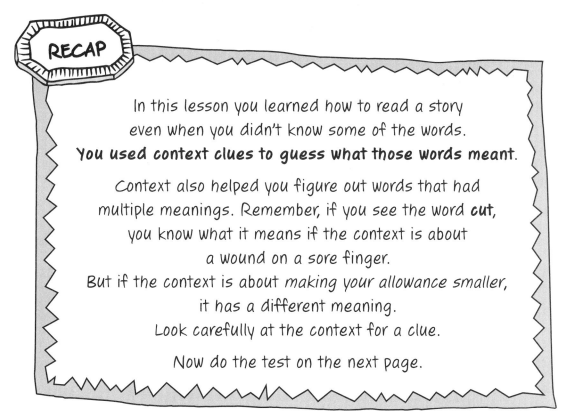

RECAP

In this lesson you learned how to read a story even when you didn't know some of the words. **You used context clues to guess what those words meant.**

Context also helped you figure out words that had multiple meanings. Remember, if you see the word **cut**, you know what it means if the context is about a wound on a sore finger.
But if the context is about *making your allowance smaller*, it has a different meaning.
Look carefully at the context for a clue.

Now do the test on the next page.

See how much you've learned. Take this test.

Test 5: Sentence Clues

Questions 1–6. Read the sentence. Choose the word that best completes the meaning of the sentence. Fill in the circle beside the answer you choose.

1. Dogs that aren't loving can growl and bite and can be very _____
   - Ⓐ round.
   - Ⓑ vicious.
   - Ⓒ funny.
   - Ⓓ light.

2. When I see such dogs I run the other way because I am _____
   - Ⓐ laughing.
   - Ⓑ too fat.
   - Ⓒ too skinny.
   - Ⓓ terrified.

3. Some animals gulp their food. Others _____ their food, taking tiny bites.
   - Ⓐ throw
   - Ⓑ drink
   - Ⓒ nibble
   - Ⓓ chase

4. The sad music made her very _____
   - Ⓐ jolly.
   - Ⓑ hungry.
   - Ⓒ unhappy.
   - Ⓓ angry.

5. He chuckled when he heard the _____ story.
   - Ⓐ excited
   - Ⓑ dull
   - Ⓒ sad
   - Ⓓ humorous

6. I could tell by his silly jacket that he had bad _____ in clothes.
   - Ⓐ socks
   - Ⓑ taste
   - Ⓒ marks
   - Ⓓ knees

GO ON

Questions 7–12. Read the two sentences. Choose the word that best fits in both sentences. Fill in the circle beside the answer you choose.

7. I could feel the wind _____. The _____ on his head hurt him.
   - Ⓐ sock
   - Ⓑ blow
   - Ⓒ song
   - Ⓓ cover

8. We sat in the _____ out of the sun. At night, the _____ covers the window.
   - Ⓐ blind
   - Ⓑ grass
   - Ⓒ chair
   - Ⓓ shade

9. Use a paper _____ to keep pages together. I will _____ your hair shorter.
   - Ⓐ ring
   - Ⓑ cut
   - Ⓒ clip
   - Ⓓ bore

10. You can tell by the red rash that he has _____. Queen bees live in _____.
    - Ⓐ houses
    - Ⓑ honey
    - Ⓒ hives
    - Ⓓ groups

11. He _____ the bread in half. She _____ in line in front of me.
    - Ⓐ made
    - Ⓑ cut
    - Ⓒ held
    - Ⓓ grabbed

12. Every _____ they pick the grapes. He can trip and _____ often.
    - Ⓐ drop
    - Ⓑ fall
    - Ⓒ spring
    - Ⓓ truck

Questions 13–15. Read the question and think about the meaning of the original word. Then choose the modern word that comes from the original word. Fill in the circle beside the word you choose.

13. Which word probably comes from the Old English word *waestum*, meaning "figure or form"?
    - Ⓐ wait
    - Ⓑ wear
    - Ⓒ waist
    - Ⓓ where

14. Which word probably comes from the Old Greek word *leukos*, meaning "bright or white"?
    - Ⓐ like
    - Ⓑ leak
    - Ⓒ lake
    - Ⓓ light

15. Which word probably comes from the Old English word *glaed*, meaning "bright and smooth"?
    - Ⓐ glove
    - Ⓑ glad
    - Ⓒ give
    - Ⓓ grove

STOP

Number Correct/Total=_____ /15

6 Main Idea and Details

Finding main idea and supporting details

How to find the **main idea** of each selection you read is the main idea of this lesson.

Read and learn to spot the difference between **details** and **main ideas**.

Here are details.

→ [Giraffes are the tallest animals in the world. They can be 19 feet tall. Some weigh more than two tons.] One ton is 2,000 pounds. How many pounds are two tons? [Wow, these are big animals!] ←— Here is the main idea.

Task 1

A giraffe's weight and height are details that add up to one main idea. Fill in the missing words that tell the main idea.

Giraffes are b _____ g a _____ _____ _____ _____ _____ s.

☞ **Feedback** This selection tells you giraffes can weigh two tons and can be 19 feet tall. These are details. They <u>add up to the main idea</u> that giraffes are *big animals*.

Task 2

The details in each item below add up to a main idea. Circle the letter of what they **add up to**.

1. If something weighs two tons (4,000 pounds), and is 19 feet high, these details **add up to** something that is _____

   A small.   B big.   C round.   D soft.

2. They smiled, laughed, tickled each other, and sang songs. These details **add up to** a time that is _____

   A happy.   B sad.   C angry.   D fearful.

3. Baked potato, roasted chicken, and root beer **add up to** a _____

   A game.   B house.   C car.   D meal.

☞ **Feedback** In one, the details add up to something *big*. Two is A, and three is D. Stories are told with **details** that add up to **a main idea**.

Task 3 Here are some more sentences about giraffes. Only one sentence tells what all the **details add up to**. That's the **main idea**. Underline the one sentence below that tells the main idea.

> These giants eat leaves. They poke their heads into trees. Then they wrap a foot-long tongue around some leaves and pull them into their mouths. They nibble their lunch. What interesting eaters they are!

☞ **Feedback** Eating leaves from trees and having long tongues that pull leaves into their mouths are interesting details. These details add up to the main idea, which is *the last sentence*.

Task 4 Here are some more selections about giraffes and some about whales. Read each one and then circle the letter of the best statement of the main idea. Don't let the <u>details</u> fool you.

1. Giraffes need water too, and that's a problem for these long-legged giants. They can't bend their legs the way we can. If you were a giraffe and your front legs didn't bend, how would you drink from a stream? Here's how giraffes do it. They stand with their front legs wide apart. Then they bend their long necks until they reach the water. That's hard work.

   A It's hard for them to drink water.   C They spread their legs.

   B They bend their necks.   D They have long necks.

2. So you think a giraffe is big! What about the blue whale? Bigger than a dinosaur, bigger than an elephant, the blue whale is longer than three classrooms end to end.

   A Dinosaurs were big.   C Elephants are like giraffes.

   B Classrooms are big.   D Whales are big.

☞ **Feedback** In one, the details about bending add up to A, the main idea. In two, you read that whales are bigger than dinosaurs, classrooms, and elephants. These details add up to the main idea of selection two, which is that *whales are big*.

3. A hundred years ago, whale hunters caught a blue whale 89 feet long. They used a crane to get part of the whale on the ship, while the rest of it dragged in the water. It was too big for the ship. The whale was 43 feet around; that may be longer than your classroom. Its jaw was 23 feet long, almost the length of three cars, and weighed over 150 tons. That's 300,000 pounds. If you weigh 75 pounds, that means the whale was as heavy as 4,000 kids like you. Now, that's heavy!

A It is too long for the ship.

B It weighs more than 4,000 kids.

C Its jaw is huge.

D Blue whales are huge.

4. The 89-foot whale had a liver that weighed 2,000 pounds. That's a ton of liver, more than enough to feed everyone in your school for the whole year. And if you think the whale's liver was big, you should have seen its tongue. It weighed 6,000 pounds! That's as much as two big trucks weigh. Can you figure how many tons that is? It had a big heart weighing in at 950 pounds, big enough for you to crawl into.

A Whale hearts are big enough to hide in.

B Whale tongues weigh three tons.

C Whales are very large animals.

D Whale livers could feed an army.

5. The whale had brown eyes and small whiskers on its chin. Its skin was clean and soft, but it was strong. All whales are strong. Once, a whale pulled a long harpoon line dragging a boat for miles. The boat tried to go backwards at full speed, but the whale was too strong. It pulled the boat forward at ten miles an hour. That's faster than most sailboats go! People have killed many whales, and very few are left. Many countries have passed laws to save whales, but whales are still in trouble. How sad it would be if all the whales died.

A Whales can pull a sailboat.

B Whale skins are clean and soft.

C Whales are special and should be saved.

D Whales are strong and have pretty eyes.

☞ **Feedback** In selection three, A, B, and C *add up to* the one main idea, which is D. In four, the main idea is C, which is what the other three choices *add up to*. And in selection five, A, B, and D are details, while C is what all the details add up to.

Read this selection and do Items One, Two, and Three.

One of my best friends is a snake. I call her Suzy. She's friendly. But I must feed her the right food. Mostly, she likes to eat fish, frogs, birds, lizards, mice, and rats. But she doesn't eat people. Snakes don't like the way people taste. But some people like the way a grilled snake tastes. Snakes are a little like those people, because snakes like the way snakes taste too.

Once two snakes tried to eat the same frog. One started at the head, and the other started at the frog's back. They met halfway down the frog, nose to nose. One snake just opened its mouth wider and kept swallowing. The other snake kept swallowing too, but it ended up being eaten. To the snake with the bigger mouth, that meal was better than a hamburger and fries.

Like all snakes, Suzy swallows her food whole. To swallow, she moves one side of herself forward, then the other side. It looks as if she crawls over her food. It also looks like hard work. Her eyes pop and her neck stretches. She keeps stopping to catch her breath.

Snakes can swallow a mouse in minutes, but they take hours to swallow something as big as a pig. Some large snakes can eat a whole goat, but it might take days or even weeks to finish the meal. So they only eat once in a while. Some eat one big meal a year. One snake in a zoo went four years with just one meal. That's a cheap snake!

It doesn't cost much to keep a snake as a pet, though most people don't like to keep pet snakes. They don't like the idea of a snake that meets another snake in the middle of a frog dinner and keeps right on eating!

1. Circle the letter of the best statement of the main idea.

    A Snakes take a week to eat.

    B Snakes are interesting animals.

    C Snakes are cheap.

    D Snakes don't eat people.

2. Circle the letter of the title that best tells the snake story's main idea.

    A "Fascinating Snakes"

    C "Cheap Eaters"

    B "Mouse Eating"

    D "Goat Eaters"

3. Here are some underlined details. Circle the letter of all those that you found in this story about snakes. Do not circle the ones that did not appear in the story, even if you know they're true.

A Snakes don't eat people.

B Most people eat snakes.

C Snakes eat hamburgers.

D Snakes can eat a dog.

E Snakes seem to swallow by crawling over their food.

☞ **Feedback** In one, B is the main idea. The others are details. A is the answer to two. In three, A and E are correct. The other details aren't in this story.

Task 6

After you read the selection, circle the letter of the best answers to the questions that follow.

You may not think so, but ice is very strong. It can hold up a heavy polar bear crossing a frozen sea. If you put bottled water outside when it's freezing, the frozen water will crack the bottle. That's because water takes up more space when it turns to ice.

Nothing can stop frozen water from pushing out. Ice can break metal water pipes or cause concrete sidewalks to crack. When rainwater falls on a mountain, it sometimes fills spaces between the rocks. If it freezes, the ice can even break the rocks.

1. All the details in this selection about ice add up to the main idea that _____

A ice can hold heavy bears.

B ice is very strong.

C frozen water can crack glass.

D even concrete is not as strong as ice.

2. Circle all the details that add up to the main idea in this story about ice.

A Ice can hold up a heavy polar bear.

B Ice can even break rocks.

C Polar bears fall through the ice.

D Ice can break pipes.

☞ **Feedback** B is the right answer to one. In two, C is the wrong answer. The other three are correct. They are the details that add up to the main idea.

Task 7 Read about desert camels. Circle the letter of the best correct answer to the three questions.

> The camel is built for the desert. Its nostrils close to keep out the sand. Its long lashes protect its eyes, and its cushioned feet are just right for walking on sand. Even the camel's hump is good for traveling in the desert. It acts as a storehouse for fat. The desert has little food, but a camel can use the stored fat for many days.
>
> Camels can carry heavy loads with their strong backs and long legs. One camel can carry 400 pounds! That's why camels are called the "cargo ships of the desert."
>
> Camel's milk is good to drink. Its meat can be eaten too. Its wool can be made into camels' hair cloth, and its hide can be used as leather. In many, many ways, the camel is useful for people who live in the desert.

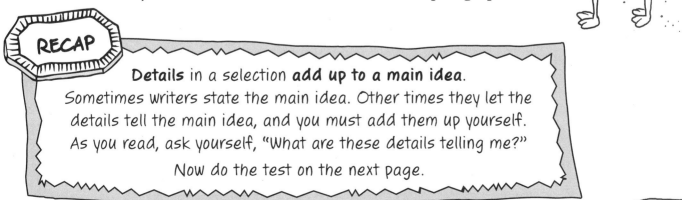

1. All the details in this selection about camels add up to a main idea which is _____

   A camel's milk is good to drink.

   B the camel's hump is good for the desert.

   C camels' hair makes good cloth.

   D the camel is built for the desert.

2. The last paragraph has four sentences. One of them is the main idea of the paragraph. Which one?

   A 1   B 2   C 3   D 4

☞ **Feedback** The main idea of the whole story is that *camels are built for the desert*. The main idea of the last paragraph is D.

RECAP

Details in a selection **add up to a main idea**. Sometimes writers state the main idea. Other times they let the details tell the main idea, and you must add them up yourself. As you read, ask yourself, "What are these details telling me?"

Now do the test on the next page.

See how much you've learned. Take this test.

Questions 1–8. Read each passage. Choose the best answer to each question. Fill in the circle beside the answer you choose.

You don't want to meet a hippo in the river. He's not a friendly fellow. The trouble is, you can't see him too well in the water. He floats just below the surface. His eyes, nose, and ears are on top of his head, just above the water line. He looks like pieces of a log floating in the river. Suddenly, he comes up at you with his mouth open. Two feet of open hippo mouth is something you want to stay away from.

Hippos can make sounds and signal one another. Unlike other animals, hippos can communicate and hear both below water and on land at the same time. No other animal can do that. And no one knows how they do it. Scientists are trying to find out. Some scientists believe the hippos' great, great, great, great, great grandparents may have been the same as dolphins. They don't look alike, but a dolphin and hippo have the same type of mouth. Maybe they hear and communicate alike too. One thing is for sure—they're not as friendly as dolphins.

Some people say hippos sweat blood. Actually, they sweat a red oil that helps heal cuts and protects them from sun rays. They also protect their skin by eating at night and staying in the water all day long.

You don't want to meet hippos on land. They are big, about eleven feet long and just under five feet tall. They weigh 5,000 to 8,000 pounds, yet they are fast runners.

1. What is the main idea of this passage?
   - Ⓐ Hippos are interesting.
   - Ⓑ Hippos talk and hear.
   - Ⓒ Hippos can be dangerous.
   - Ⓓ Hippos swim all day and feed all night.

2. What is the hippos' red sweat?
   - Ⓐ a way to talk underwater and on land
   - Ⓑ an oil to protect the skin
   - Ⓒ something they got from dolphins
   - Ⓓ a fuel to help them run fast

3. Why are hippos tough to see in the river?
   - Ⓐ They hide in bushes.
   - Ⓑ They are shy.
   - Ⓒ They move so fast.
   - Ⓓ They look like floating logs.

4. What is the best title for this passage?
   - Ⓐ "Diving for the Attack"
   - Ⓑ "The Friendly Hippo"
   - Ⓒ "Playing with Dolphins"
   - Ⓓ "The Interesting Hippo"

GO ON

In a country where presidents have always been men, Americans were surprised in 1972 when Shirley Chisholm, a woman, said, "I want to be president. I will run for that office." And she did. She didn't win. But she showed the country that an African American woman could make a difference in the way men tried to run the country.

In New York, before running for president, Ms. Chisholm ran for and won a seat in the U.S. Congress. She was the first African American Congresswoman. At first, the men in Congress didn't take much notice of her. She was never called on to speak. So one day, she walked to the front of Congress and gave a short speech. Everyone listened. After that day, they always listened to "The Lady from New York."

When Ms. Chisholm ran for president, people heard "The Lady from New York" all over the country. However, she had to drop out of the race because it cost too much money. So she returned to Congress. This time, everyone wanted to hear her speak. Here was someone who spoke well and had been smart enough to run for president.

---

5. This is a true story that is mostly about _____
   Ⓐ running for president in New York.
   Ⓑ running for Congress in New York.
   Ⓒ a woman who ran for president.
   Ⓓ African American men in Congress.

6. Shirley Chisholm is also known for being the first _____
   Ⓐ African American woman in Congress.
   Ⓑ person to run for president.
   Ⓒ woman to ever run for Congress.
   Ⓓ woman who ever spoke to Congress.

7. What is the main idea of this story?
   Ⓐ how an African American spoke in Congress
   Ⓑ how New York sent her to Congress
   Ⓒ the cost of running for president
   Ⓓ the first African American woman to run for president

8. What is the best title for this passage?
   Ⓐ "A Woman Who Dared Be First"
   Ⓑ "Giving a Short Speech"
   Ⓒ "The Cost of Running for President"
   Ⓓ "Speaking in Congress"

STOP

Number Correct/Total=_____ /8

7 Constructing Meaning

Identifying sequence and cause and effect and drawing conclusions

Good readers remember the **sequence of events** in a story.
Sequence means <u>order</u>,
and **events** are <u>what happen</u> in a story.

Also, knowing the order in which things happen
helps you understand what makes, or **causes**,
an event or an **effect**.

Task 1

Read the selection and then circle the letters of the right answers.

Jasmine was waiting outside. "Come on. We'll be late," she yelled at Trish, who was finishing breakfast. Trish drank the whole glass of milk in two gulps. She ran out the door to meet her friend and started to cough. She had drunk the milk too fast.

1. Which event came first?   A drank the milk   B coughed

2. Which event came last?   A drank the milk   B coughed

3. The **order** in which events happen is important if you want to know what **causes** something to happen. What caused Trish to cough?

   A She drank the milk too fast.

   B She drank a whole glass of milk.

☞ **Feedback** In one, first she *drank the milk,* A; then she *coughed.* So the answer to two is B. In three, *drinking milk too fast* **caused** her to *cough.* So the answer to three is A. *Cough* is the **effect** and *drinking too fast* is the **cause**. The cause comes before the effect. If someone asks, "Why did she cough?" your answer is, "Be**cause** she drank the milk too fast."

Circle the letters of the correct answers.

1. What causes you to sleep?

   A You're rested.   B You're tired.   C You're hungry.

2. What is an effect of being tired?

   A sleep   B jumping   C hunger

3. You are sleepy because _____

   A you're tired.   B you're rested.   C it's dark.

4. The cause is sleep. What is the effect?

   A tired   B rested   C hunger

☞ **Feedback** Now you know that **causes come before effects**. In one, being *tired*, B, causes you to sleep. In two, *sleep* is an effect of being tired. In three, you're sleepy because *you're tired*, A. In four, sleep causes you to be *rested*, B. In the sequence of events, causes come before effects. Thirst causes you to drink water. You drink because you are thirsty. Drinking is the effect of thirst and comes after being thirsty.

First, read this sad story. Then circle the letter of the correct answer for each of the four questions that follow.

Mr. Davis saw the baby deer was in great pain. He couldn't tell if his car had hurt her, but he knew that she needed help. Gently he placed her in a box and took her to the animal doctor. The doctor fixed her leg and dressed her cuts. In one short month, the deer became a healthy member of the Davis family. Jeff and Janet, the Davis children, named their new pet Maya after a famous poet.

Maya ate at the kitchen table. She had her own bed and a pen that was her play yard. Kids came from all over the town to play with Maya. She played tag with the kids and even went to school one day with Jeff. He brought her for show-and-tell. Maya loved to play with Winston, the Davis dog, and with Sunshine, the neighbor's black cat.

One day, the county animal officer came to the house. "It's against the law," he said, "to keep a wild animal. The law says she must be free."

"But she's not wild," explained Mrs. Davis. "She's as tame as our dog and the neighbor's cat. Sometimes I think she is tamer than Jeff or Janet," she said with a wink at her two children.

The wink didn't work. The men from the county animal office stuffed Maya into a cage on the back of a truck. Poor, frightened Maya struggled to escape, but the cage door closed and the truck drove off to the woods to set her free.

The next day, Mrs. Davis heard the sad news. Maya was so upset that she died in the truck. The Davis family was angry. The county animal officers called to say how sorry they were too, though none of the tears brought Maya back.

1. Why does Mr. Davis put the baby deer in the box?

    A The county animal office had called.

    B The deer is hurt.

    C The deer doesn't want to go home.

    D Mr. Davis is lonely.

2. What is the effect of Maya's visit to the doctor?

    A She is hurt.   C She cries.

    B She gets better.   D She winks at Jeff.

3. The county animal officer comes to the house because _____

    A the children make too much noise.

    B Maya eats off the kitchen table.

    C Maya plays with Jeff and Janet.

    D it's against the law to have a pet deer.

4. What is the effect of putting Maya in the cage on the truck?

    A She runs away.   C The animal officer comes.

    B She dies.   D It is against the law.

☞ **Feedback** A why question, like question one, is looking for a cause. In one, Mr. Davis puts the baby deer in a box *because she is hurt*. In two, the doctor's care *causes her to get better*. Getting better is the effect of good doctoring. The officer comes because *it is against the law to have a pet deer*. In four, putting poor Maya in the cage *causes her to die*.

Read these two selections about volcanoes then answer the questions that follow each selection. Circle the letters of the <u>best</u> answers. Look out! There may be more than one possible answer, but you must select the best.

Deep below the ground the earth is hot. Thousands of miles below where we walk, the earth is so hot that it melts rocks. Melted rock is called lava. The lava boils like water. Sometimes, the lava finds a crack in the earth and boils to the surface. It becomes a volcano.

When the lava comes out, it flows along until it cools and becomes rock. Can you imagine that some of the rocks and boulders you see were once boiling lava? After the old lava hardens, new lava may seep out of the cracks and flow over the old lava. We get layers of solid rock. Sometimes when we cut into hillsides to build roads, we can see volcanic layers of rock.

1. What causes the lava to come to the surface of the earth?

   A   It cracks.   C   It cuts hillsides.
   B   It boils up.   D   It makes layers.

2. What is the effect of new lava flowing over old lava?

   A   volcanoes   C   boiling
   B   cracks in the earth   D   layers of rock

3. What causes lava to become rock?

   A   cracking   C   melting
   B   flowing   D   cooling

4. What comes first in the making of a volcano?

   A   melted rock   C   building roads
   B   cut into hillsides   D   layers of rock

☞ **Feedback** In one, *boiling* causes lava to surface. Two and three are both D. In four, volcanoes start from *melted rock*, A. Do you see how the sequence in which these events happen often tells you the cause or the effect?

Sometimes the lava cools and hardens in the crack. Then the lava can't flow anymore. The cooled lava is like a plug in a bottle. The plug keeps the lava from flowing out of the earth. It's like holding down the lid on a boiling pot. Deep down, the boiling lava pushes and pushes on the plug. Then one day the boiling lava pushes so hard that it bursts into the air in a huge explosion. The explosion shoots burning lava as high as the clouds. The lava cools and falls as rocks and ash all around the opening.

Over many years a great hole forms from the erupting lava and ash. The hole is called a crater, which is where the lava first burst from the ground. The crater grows and grows as the volcano hurls more and more lava into the air. Some craters are many miles wide and hundreds of feet deep.

When a volcano explodes, gas comes out with the lava. Most of this gas is steam, like the steam from a boiling teakettle. In the air the steam cools. Cooled steam becomes water droplets. The droplets collect in great white clouds that hang over hot volcano tops. In some volcanoes, steam escapes all the time. Those volcanoes have clouds over them every day.

5. What causes volcanoes to explode?

   A   ashes in the air

   B   plugged up lava cracks

   C   ash piled up around the crater

   D   new layers of cooled lava

6. What causes rocks, lava, and ashes to fly through the air?

   A   explosion

   B   air currents

   C   cooling

   D   crack

7. What causes volcano craters?

   A   many trees

   B   erupting lava and ash

   C   steam from deep in the earth

   D   clouds high in the sky

☞ **Feedback** In five, the explosion is caused by *the plug that blocks lava flow*, B. In six, A is correct. The *explosion* causes rocks and ashes to fly through the air. In seven, the crater is caused by *many eruptions*, B.

When you think about the **sequence of events**, you can make a decision or form an opinion about what has happened. You can decide that what a character did was right or wrong. You can decide what a chacter **is like**!

You can **draw conclusions**!

Read the selection and circle the letters of the best correct answers.

Near the cave entrance was a large rock that blocked most of the rain and wind. Peter turned to the old wolf that shivered outside next to the rock. "Okay," he said. "You can come in. I don't think you're as friendly as a dog, but you don't look as vicious as a hungry wolf should look. Come on in. I won't hurt you."

The wolf was licking the knife wound on his right hip. He kept one eye on Peter. He eyed the warm fire and shivered as the rain fell on him and his bleeding hip. But he would not move closer to the warm fire. If Peter moved toward him, the wolf backed away. So Peter just sat quietly by the warm fire, waiting.

1. The writer doesn't tell us, but we can conclude from the knife wound that the wolf had _____

   A   a fight with another wolf.   C   hurt itself on the sharp rocks.

   B   a fight with a human being.   D   chased Peter into the cave.

2. You can conclude that the wolf _____

   A   was not afraid of Peter.   C   did not want to get warm.

   B   was afraid of Peter.   D   knew Peter.

3. The story doesn't tell us, but what might Peter be waiting for?

   A   the fire to go out   C   the wolf to come

   B   something to eat   D   the wolf to go away

☞ **Feedback** The answers are B, B, C.

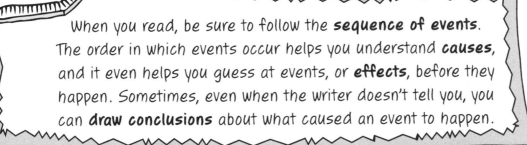

RECAP

When you read, be sure to follow the **sequence of events**. The order in which events occur helps you understand **causes**, and it even helps you guess at events, or **effects**, before they happen. Sometimes, even when the writer doesn't tell you, you can **draw conclusions** about what caused an event to happen.

Test 7: Consructing Meaning

Questions 1–10. Read each passage. Choose the best answer to each question. Fill in the circle beside the answer you choose.

When the North and South went to war in this country, some children were only nine or ten when they became soldiers. They were called drummer boys, and they used their drums to signal orders to the soldiers. Drummers woke the troops at dawn by signaling on their drums that it was time to wake up. They led marches, and sometimes they led soldiers into battle. They carried drums, not guns, but they marched in front of the troops.

An army officer always kept his drummer boy nearby. Sometimes things did not go well. If the army had to fall back, the drum gave the order. Sometimes the drummer boy beat his drumsticks. That meant, "Charge!"

During a battle, drummer boys took care of soldiers who were hurt. When a soldier was shot, drummer boys carried the soldier to the hospitals.

Two drummer boys became very famous compared to others. One boy from Ohio was only nine years old and spent four years in the war. When he was old enough, he became a real soldier and served 55 years in the army. Another drummer boy was only eleven years old when he got a medal from President Lincoln.

1. Drummer boys were _____
   Ⓐ good fighters.
   Ⓑ young children.
   Ⓒ older than the fighters.
   Ⓓ playing music.

2. How did soldiers know when to charge?
   Ⓐ They got telephone messages.
   Ⓑ They were awakened in the morning.
   Ⓒ They were told by the nurses.
   Ⓓ They were signaled by the drumsticks.

3. Drummer boys probably _____
   Ⓐ saw terrible sights.
   Ⓑ were officers.
   Ⓒ fought hard.
   Ⓓ ran away.

4. Officers kept drummer boys nearby to _____
   Ⓐ feed the horses.
   Ⓑ shine their shoes.
   Ⓒ listen to their music.
   Ⓓ signal the soldiers.

5. Today, most nine- and ten-year-olds _____
   Ⓐ are better drummers.
   Ⓑ are working on farms.
   Ⓒ are in school.
   Ⓓ are girls, not boys.

GO ON

"No! No, Maxine. Don't touch that worm," Terry Tuna cried out. "If you bite, you'll end up on a dish! You'll never get home if you nibble that worm," Terry told her. "There's a hook, line, rod, and a person at the other end. You'll end up in someone's belly."

"It's not right for people to hang their hooks down here," said Maxine. "We should teach those people a lesson or two."

"Why not?" asked Terry. "You work at a school. A whole school of mackerel should be able to think of something to do." Then Terry grinned. Fish have funny grins. "Let's teach those people a lesson. Bring me your whole school. If people go *fishing*, then fish will go *peopling*."

"We'll go what? We'll go where?" Maxine didn't understand Terry.

"People go *fishing*. So fish should go *peopling*. We'll show those people!"

When the school of mackerel arrived, Terry stood them on top of each other. At the top, a mackerel stuck his tail out of the water.

"Fish! Fish!" a man yelled. He dived into the water to grab the fish. Instead, all the mackerel grabbed the man. They pulled him to Oliver Octopus, who put him on a people dish. Then all the mackerel yelled, "Let's eat. Man, oh man, this looks better than worms."

Well, fish don't like the way people taste, so they let him go. The poor man swam away faster than a fish. When he told his story to all the other people, they called it "a fish story," but they stopped fishing.

6. From the context, you can conclude that Maxine _____

    Ⓐ doesn't know about fishing.

    Ⓑ knows a lot about fishing.

    Ⓒ is not Terry's friend.

    Ⓓ is bigger than Terry.

7. If Maxine swallowed the juicy worm, what would the effect be?

    Ⓐ She would be hungry.

    Ⓑ She would eat more worms.

    Ⓒ She would end up in a belly.

    Ⓓ She would be a student.

8. The man on the plate feels _____

    Ⓐ funny.   Ⓒ lost.

    Ⓑ hungry.   Ⓓ afraid.

9. Why don't the fish eat the man?

    Ⓐ He is too big to swallow.

    Ⓑ Fish don't like how people taste.

    Ⓒ Oliver won't let them.

    Ⓓ They have to go back to school.

10. In this story, which of these events happened first?

    Ⓐ Maxine wants to eat a worm.

    Ⓑ Maxine brings her school of mackerel.

    Ⓒ Oliver holds the man on a plate.

    Ⓓ The man swims away fast.

STOP

Number Correct/Total=_____ /10

8 Evaluating Information

Telling the diference between fiction and nonfiction and between fact and opinion

> Writers can have strong feelings about their subjects.
> This is called **writer's viewpoint.**
> The viewpoint can be **for** or **against** something.
>
> Look for a writer's viewpoint when you read.

Task 1

Read these two selections then circle the letters of the correct answers.

Not long ago, our air was sweet and clean. Birds flew peacefully through bright blue skies. The only smoke in the sky came from campfires and log cabins.

As our nation grew, factories and cars soon filled our skies with ugly smoke. Today we are in great danger because our skies are filled with poisons.

1. The writer thinks _____
   A birds still fly in blue skies.
   B our air is still clean.
   C our nation is in danger.
   D we should have no campfires.

2. This writer seems to want _____
   A more factories.
   B more campfires.
   C more cars.
   D less smoke and poison.

When I use a dictionary, I discover more than a word's meaning. If I look up the word *sandwich*, I discover that putting food on bread was what the Earl of *Sandwich* did 200 years ago when he was playing cards. He didn't want to stop for meals. The sandwich was named after him.

3. You can guess the writer _____
   A plays cards.
   B is interested in words.
   C eats many sandwiches.
   D wants fast meals.

☞ **Feedback** In one, you can tell the writer is upset because she thinks *our nation is in danger* from poisons in the air. She probably wants *less smoke and poisons*, D, in two. In three, you can conclude that the writer *finds words interesting*. Do you like words?

> The word for **a made-up story** is **fiction**.
> A **fiction writer** invents stories.
> Some **fiction stories** could be true, but aren't.
> Some **stories** could never be true.
>
> True stories are <u>not fiction</u>,
> which is why true stories are called **<u>non</u>fiction**.

Task 2

Learn how to spot the difference between **fiction** and **nonfiction**. Read each selection and then circle the correct answers to the questions.

> A glider has no motor. It rises by soaring on warm air. It comes down on cold air. Warm air rises; cool air sinks. That is why, in a house, it is warmer near the ceiling and cooler near the floor.
>
> The glider cannot rise from the ground by itself. It needs an airplane to pull it into the air. Once in the air, though, it moves smoothly and safely with the warm and cool breezes. What a peaceful and gentle ride!

1. This selection is _____

   poetry.   song.   fiction.   nonfiction.

Please don't pick me!

> Patty turned to the yellow flower and said, "You're the color of sunshine. You make me smile."
>
> "Thank you," said the jolly yellow flower. "You're very kind. But please don't pick me, or any of my flower family. We like it here in the ground."

2. This story could _____   really happen.   not really happen.

3. This story is _____   fiction.   nonfiction.

☞ **Feedback** In one, you can tell the writer likes gliders in this *nonfiction* story. In two, a talking flower could *not really happen*. That's why the selection in which the yellow flower talks must be *fiction*.

Some stories are obviously **fiction**.
Animals talking and green people from outer space
are good clues something is fiction.
Some stories seem very real, but they are still stories.

In **nonfiction**, details seem to be really true.

Task 3

Read these six selections looking for fiction or nonfiction clues. Circle the correct answers.

1. "I'm from Mars," a voice squeaked from a purple flower in its belly. At least it looked like a belly, but the mouth was his belly button and his belly button was his mouth.

   fiction   nonfiction

2. The pretty ladybug caught in the huge spider web cried for mercy.

   fiction   nonfiction

3. Mother elephants carry a calf for 24 months before birth.

   fiction   nonfiction

4. Pioneers crossed oceans to discover new lands. They crossed rivers and mountains in discovering America.

   fiction   nonfiction

BOOM! BOOM! BOOM!

5. The sound the woodpecker made on the dead tree trunk was as loud as a drumbeat. All the animals heard it for miles around. Within minutes, an army of brave friends gathered to protect the lost children.

   fiction   nonfiction

6. Mostly found in the Far East, pagodas are sacred temples where people pray.

   fiction   nonfiction

👉 **Feedback** The first two selections are *fiction*. Voices don't come from belly buttons, and ladybugs can't really cry for mercy. The next two selections are *nonfiction*. The facts sound true. Selection five is *fiction*, of course, and selection six describes a true place of worship, so it is *nonfiction*.

Facts are true statements. You can have **opinions** about facts.

It may be a **fact** that the sun is shining.
If a writer says the sun is too hot, that's an **opinion**.
Someone else may think the same sun is not hot enough.
A basketball player may be six feet, five inches tall. That's a **fact**.
A seven-foot-tall player may think six feet, five inches is small.
That's an **opinion**.

Task 4

Write **F** for *fact* or **O** for *opinion* on the line after each numbered sentence. Three are done for you.

1. Orbit means a *path around something*. __F__ 2. As the earth orbits

the sun, the seasons change. __F__ 3. Those changes are interesting. __O__

4. The sun has a different effect on the earth at different points in the

orbit. _____ 5. That's what makes the seasons. _____ 6. When the sun

shines on us a lot, we say it is summer. _____ 7. That's when it's too hot for

me. _____ 8. I believe that spring and fall are more comfortable. _____

9. It takes about 365 days for the earth to move around the sun. _____

10. That's a long time to travel through space. _____ 11. But the earth has

been traveling that orbit for millions of years. _____

☞ **Feedback** A word's definition is a fact. So sentence one is a *fact*. In two, the *fact* is that the orbit does cause seasons to change. But if someone thinks those changes are interesting, that's a person's *opinion*. Numbers four, five, and six are *facts*. Temperature is a *fact* too, but to call a temperature too hot or too cold is an *opinion*. In number eight, a person's belief is an *opinion*. A year is 365 days, a fact, but whether or not a year is a long time is an *opinion*. In eleven, it's a *fact* that the earth has been traveling in its orbit for millions of years.

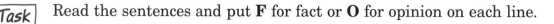

Task 5

Read the sentences and put **F** for fact or **O** for opinion on each line.

1. The nest has four eagles. _____

2. Eagles are ugly birds. _____

3. The bus is fun to ride. _____

4. Your hair's too long. _____

5. There are clouds in the sky. _____

6. The bus goes 55 miles an hour. _____

7. Boys should not climb mountains. _____

☞ **Feedback** In one, the number of eagles is a *fact*, but in two, how they look is an *opinion*. Three, what someone thinks about a bus ride, and four, the length of your hair, are o*pinions*. Five and six are *facts*, and seven is an *opinion*. What's your opinion of this Task?

Task 6

This time circle **Fact** or **Opinion** to describe each sentence.

1. At nine o'clock the boat left the dock.   **Fact**   **Opinion**

2. Wild Willy and Tame Tom were friends.   **Fact**   **Opinion**

3. Her mother is a great cook.   **Fact**   **Opinion**

4. We should vote for Clancy. He's smart.   **Fact**   **Opinion**

☞ **Feedback** One and two are *facts*, but three and four are *opinions*.

Task 7

In the next three selections, spot the writers' points of view. They are either true or made-up stories. Circle the letters of the answers.

> Mrs. Cerf's five-year-old son, Chris, went to a party in a brand-new suit. When the boy got home, his new suit was full of holes. Someone had cut the holes with scissors. "What happened to your new suit?" asked his surprised mother.
>
> "We played supermarket," Chris said. "And I was the Swiss cheese."

1. The writer wants you to find the ending of the Cerf story very _____

   A sad.   B funny.   C educational.

2. His story was probably _____

   A true.   B made up.   C either true or made up.

   Millions of kids go to sleep hungry every night. For only three dollars a week, you can feed one of them. You can make him or her feel better when he/she climbs into bed. If many people will send just three dollars a week, we can feed thousands of these children.

3. The writer wants people to _____

   A give money.   B eat more.

4. The writer is probably telling a _____

   A true story.   B made-up story.

   For many people, getting somewhere on time is the hardest thing to do. Nature doesn't have that problem. Each year since the beginning of time summer begins about June 21, and winter begins about December 22.

5. The writer is no doubt telling a _____

   A true story.   B made-up story.

☞ **Feedback** The answer to one is B. In two, it is possible that the story is *made up*, but it is also possible that it is *true*; it's hard to tell. Let's say the correct answer is C. In three, the writer's point of view is very clear, *give money*. And in four, television news programs show the world's hungry children all the time. So the story is *true*. In the last selection, the answer is A, a *true story*.

RECAP

All writers have **points of view**, and you will often want to make a good guess as to why the writer wrote her or his story.

To be a good reader, it's important to spot the difference between **fiction** and **nonfiction** and between **fact** and **opinion**.

Test 8: Evaluating Information

Questions 1–10. Read each selection. Then choose the best answer to each question. Fill in the circle beside the answer you choose.

"I don't like this place." Tracy stamped her foot. "Maybe it's a friendly town, but not to me. We moved in 18 hours ago, and no one has come to play with me. No one has even said, 'Welcome to Pleasantville.' I don't think Pleasantville is so pleasant."

Her mother was moving a table to the other side of the room. Isaac was gazing out the window. He said nothing, but he was thinking about the city where they used to live.

"In the city, everyone was our friend." Tracy was talking to herself loud enough for everyone else to hear. "I couldn't go down the stairs without meeting a friend. I couldn't sit for ten minutes in the kitchen before some friend was at the door asking me to come over and play. Now I'm all alone."

"C'mon, Tracy," Isaac was smiling. "Give it a few days. We don't know anyone yet. We'll find friends. Let's go out and look for some."

They stepped out the front door and almost tripped over Cato. Cato was the white cat that lived next door. But Tracy and Isaac didn't know that. They had never had a cat. In the big building they had just moved from, no animals were allowed. Tracy was afraid. She just stood still. She had never patted a cat.

Cato rubbed up against Tracy's right leg. Then the cat rolled on to his side and lay half on the top step and half on Tracy's shoe. Tracy didn't dare move. Isaac smiled.

---

1. What is the writer's viewpoint?
   - Ⓐ sad for Tracy
   - Ⓑ angry at Pleasantville
   - Ⓒ caring about this family
   - Ⓓ in favor of Tracy

2. When Tracy says that Pleasantville isn't so pleasant, she is stating _____
   - Ⓐ a fact.
   - Ⓑ an opinion.
   - Ⓒ the truth.
   - Ⓓ a joke.

3. Tracy is upset mostly because _____
   - Ⓐ she doesn't have a cat.
   - Ⓑ her mother doesn't speak to her.
   - Ⓒ Isaac is angry.
   - Ⓓ she has no new friends yet.

4. Which sentence is a fact?
   - Ⓐ Tracy should be more patient.
   - Ⓑ This is the start of an interesting story.
   - Ⓒ Cato rubbed up against her leg.
   - Ⓓ Isaac certainly has common sense.

GO ON

If good fiction is meant to be like real life, then it should not be all sad or all happy. Even when a life is mostly sad, it has some happy times. That's what makes this play so good. It is both funny and sad.

The name of the play is *Teddy Takes a Tumble*. Teddy is unhappy, but every now and then, some funny things happen. In one part of the play, he studies hard for the wrong test. When he finds that the test is in English, not math, he trips and falls into the pool just before test time. His teacher sends him home for a change of clothes, and he does not have to take the test that day.

The actor playing Teddy is very good. Teddy's mother is played by Annie Croft, who looks like a mom even though she is only ten years old.

---

5. The writer wrote this selection mainly to _____
   Ⓐ tell us about a play she saw.
   Ⓑ make us cry.
   Ⓒ tell us how funny the play was.
   Ⓓ make us buy something.

6. Which sentence tells us about good fiction?
   Ⓐ "The name of the play is *Teddy Takes a Tumble*."
   Ⓑ "The actor playing Teddy is very good."
   Ⓒ "His teacher sends him home for a change of clothes . . ."
   Ⓓ It "is meant to be like real life . . ."

7. Which sentence is a fact?
   Ⓐ "The actor playing Teddy is good."
   Ⓑ "Some funny things happen."
   Ⓒ "The name of the play . . ."
   Ⓓ The play is so good.

8. Which sentence is an opinion?
   Ⓐ The girl who plays Mom is ten years old.
   Ⓑ His teacher sent him home for a change of clothes.
   Ⓒ He studies hard for the wrong test.
   Ⓓ Annie Croft looks like a mom.

9. What is the writer's opinion about *Teddy Takes a Tumble*?
   Ⓐ It is sad.
   Ⓑ It is happy.
   Ⓒ It is a good play.
   Ⓓ It is not a very good play.

10. The writer's viewpoint about the play is _____
   Ⓐ friendly.
   Ⓑ angry.
   Ⓒ sad.
   Ⓓ bored.

STOP

Number Correct/Total=_____ /10

9 Characters and Plot

Understanding characters and plot in a story

Most stories are about people.
Some are about animals that think and act like people.
Characters in a story **do, say, think,** and **feel** things
that help make the **plot** of the story.
To understand what happens in a story,
you must understand the **characters** and the **plot**.

Look for clues that tell you about the characters in a story.

Task 1

Read about these characters and then circle the best answers to the questions.

Sir Blunderdud sat in his saddle looking down into the town below.

"Oh, what a happy day," said Blunderdud to Drexel, his faithful dragon. "Tomorrow I will marry the lady of my dreams, proud Princess Priscilla."

"What a great day it will be," said Drexel. "Can I wear a fancy tuxedo? I'm naturally good-looking, you know."

Sir Blunderdud was too busy thinking good thoughts to hear Drexel. Blunderdud almost never heard other people.

1. Which line in the story is a clue to Sir Blunderdud's **character**?

   A "Oh, what a happy day."

   B Blunderdud almost never heard other people.

2. What does Drexel say that's a clue to his character?

   A "Can I wear a fancy tuxedo?"

   B "I'm naturally good-looking, you know."

☞ **Feedback** You decided that Blunderdud *doesn't pay attention to people*, and that Drexel *thinks about how he looks*. Did you find those clues?

You can begin to guess this story's **plot**, or **what happens in a story**.

Somehow, a marriage, a silly dragon, and a foolish knight who doesn't hear what others say will make things happen and do things as the story unfolds.

Task 2

Read more of the story. Then circle the best answer to each question.

"She'll be here soon," said Sir Blunderdud. "Dragons breathe fire. So, Drexel, I want you to breathe big fireworks to welcome her. Something fancy!"

Drexel looked sadly at his master. "You know, I'd really like to help you out. But I have a head cold. My drippy nose keeps putting out my dragon fire."

Not listening, Blunderdud kept talking. He was too busy thinking good thoughts. "Your fireworks will be super. I'll have twenty dancing sea horses, a cupcake maker, and four pairs of candle dippers to sing love songs. All you must do is breathe her name in flames across the night sky: **WELCOME PRISCILLA.**"

"But, blut, blot, blat . . ." Poor Drexel could not say words. His nose was dripping and got in the way of his tongue, and his master was not listening anyway.

1. Blunderdud doesn't hear Drexel because Blunderdud is _____

   A not nice.

   B self-centered.

   C deaf.

   D too busy.

2. The plot begins to get interesting when Drexel says he can't make fireworks because _____

   A he has a cold.

   B he is tired.

   C Sir Blunderdud doesn't listen.

   D he doesn't like cupcakes.

3. You can tell that Drexel wants to help Blunderdud when the story says that _____

   A Blunderdud isn't listening.

   B Drexel is sad.

   C Drexel's drips get in the way.

   D Blunderdud keeps talking.

👉 **Feedback** A story's plot is the sequence of events that follow each other. First, you meet the main characters, Blunderdud and Drexel. You see what they're like. *Blunderdud is self-centered,* so he doesn't hear what Drexel says, the answer to one, and Drexel *has a cold*, the answer to two. Drexel is afraid his drippy nose won't let him breathe fire. *Drexel is sad* because he thinks he may not be able to help, the answer to three.

Task 3 Read the last part of the story and then circle the letters of the best right answers.

"Here she comes! Priscilla is coming!" cried the village guard. This was a friendly town. That's why the guard called the princess by her first name. Priscilla stepped from her wagon. Sir Blunderdud gave the signal, and the welcome began.

Twenty sea horses whirled and twirled on tiny tails. For seven minutes they danced without stopping for breath. Then the crowd really went wild when the cupcake maker baked and iced 300 white, brown, and pink cupcakes. The candle dippers dipped their candles and sang love songs. Then came Drexel's big moment. He did not know whether he could do it.

He took a great breath, warmed up his flamer, and let out a mighty puff. A flame shot from his drippy nostrils. It turned his drip to steam.

"Hot dragon fire!" cried a happy Drexel. "I'm really skywriting!" He puffed out the letters, one after the other, as the crowd cheered.

Oh my! What happened? Suddenly Drexel forgot how to spell Priscilla. Everyone was silent. They waited and waited. Even Sir Blunderdud stopped thinking good thoughts. Drexel's nose began to drip. It started to itch. His eyes filled up. And then a big explosion!

Drexel sneezed. The crowd went wild. Sir Blunderdud cheered. Priscilla smiled. Drexel had sneezed a huge ball of dragon fire that said

Drexel was a hero.

1. Does Drexel's cold stop him from making his dragon fire?

   Yes　　　No

2. What causes Drexel to stop in the middle of Priscilla's name?

   A He forgets how to spell her name.　　C He can't breathe.

   B He is looking for his tuxedo.　　D He sneezes.

3. How does Drexel finally write her name?

   A Blunderdud helps him.　　C The cupcake maker helps him.

   B Candle dippers sing songs.　　D Drexel sneezes.

☞ **Feedback** Isn't the plot interesting? That's because the storyteller makes interesting characters like Drexel and Blunderdud. Then the storyteller has the characters do one interesting thing after another. The story builds to a high point. In this story, *Drexel's head cold does not stop his fire*, the answer to one. In this story, the high point is when Drexel *forgets how to spell Priscilla's name*, the answer to two. Sometimes the events trick us. Drexel's cold helps him *sneeze* out her name, the answer to three.

Task 4

Here are the beginnings of two stories. Read the selections and then see whether you can spot the clues that help the plot unfold in each story. Circle the letter of the best answer.

A king of the North Land had seven sons. He sent six of the sons to find wives, but he kept his youngest son, who dearly loved his brothers, at home.

"Take my finest horses and clothes of gold and silver. Each of you bring back a wife and bring an extra one for your youngest brother. He will stay with me."

After many months, the brothers found a king who had six pretty daughters. The sons fell in love with the daughters. They forgot all about a seventh wife for the seventh brother that was left behind. Love sometimes does that—it makes us forgetful.

On the way home, they passed a giant's house. He saw them coming, growled at them, and turned them all to stone. Horses, princes, and princesses became stone statues in the giant's backyard.

When the youngest son heard what happened, he jumped on his horse and . . .

1. You can guess that the writer tells you these things because the _____

   A story will end with everyone turned to stone.

   B youngest brother will have to find a way to get his brothers back.

   C king will die of a broken heart.

   D king will find a new wife and have seven more sons.

2. You can tell the giant was not a good guy by such clues as _____

   A they forgot about their younger brother.

   B the brothers had lots of fine horses and fine clothes.

   C the giant saw them coming.

   D the giant growled at them.

👉 **Feedback** From the way the writer begins the plot, you can tell the *seventh son will have to rescue his selfish brothers*, the answer to one. You know from the one word *growl*, that the giant is not a nice guy! With just one or two words, a writer lets us know a lot about a character.

Many years ago a poor, frightened farmer worked day and night. He woke up poor, worked all day poor, and went to sleep poor. His father was poor, as was his father's father.

Many people are poor, but this man did nothing about it. He just blamed everyone else, even the god of riches, Nyambi. One day Nyambi heard him and decided to teach him a lesson. So he brought the poor farmer to his heavenly village. All the poor man's ancestors were there.

"You say that being poor is what you must be because your family was always poor," said Nyambi. "Since you're so unhappy, I'll let you change families. Pick a family that you want to be a part of."

3. In this new story, the plot builds around two characters.

   They are _____.

4. We have a clue to the plot when Nyambi decides to

   _____.

5. The poor man blames his poverty on Nyambi and

   _____.

☞ **Feedback** The two characters are the god of riches, *Nyambi*, and the *poor man*, the answer to three. We know that the story will be about how to *teach the poor man a lesson*, the answer to four. A good reader is thinking: *What will that lesson be*? The lesson will have something to do with blaming being poor *on his own family*, the answer to five. Now read the rest of the story to see what unfolds.

> The poor man looked at all the families. He could choose to be part of a rich or a poor family, or part of a family somewhere in between rich and poor. But the man was so afraid to try something new that when he saw his own poor family, he chose them over all the other choices.

6. The man chose his own family because _____
   A he didn't have many choices.
   B he had too many choices.
   C Nyambi punished him.
   D he was afraid to try something new.

7. What lesson can you take away from this folktale?
   A Once you are poor, you will always be poor.
   B Don't choose another family.
   C Don't make Nyambi angry.
   D Don't be afraid to try something new.

☞ **Feedback** D and D are the correct answers.

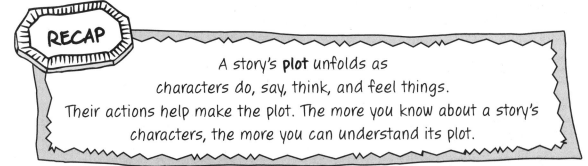

RECAP

A story's **plot** unfolds as
characters do, say, think, and feel things.
Their actions help make the plot. The more you know about a story's
characters, the more you can understand its plot.

See how much you've learned. Take this test.

Test 9: Characters and Plot

Questions 1–10. Read the selection. Then choose the best answer to each question. Fill in the circle beside the answers you choose.

Isabella's eyes were big to begin with. When she saw the tiny boat though, her eyes almost popped out of her head.

"Is that going to carry me and my suitcase?" she asked the little man who held the boat steady against the waves. He said nothing. He just dropped the suitcase into the water and let it sink. Then he held out his hand to help her aboard.

"Oops," she said to herself. "I guess not. Just the two of us and that silly little motor in a rubber boat." It wasn't much bigger than the bed she had slept in a week ago. Since then, she had been sleeping in the woods. Soldiers were looking for her. She did not dare go to a hotel. That morning she had washed in the river water. She had to crack through the thin ice to get enough water to wash. Now, fourteen hours later, she was trying to sneak across choppy waters in a tiny rubber boat.

The tiny motor seemed as silent as the man who started it up. It did not roar like most motors. Nor did it hum like some she had heard. This one just went putt-putt and sounded as slow as the boat seemed to move.

Not twenty feet from shore, she was already soaked with icy water. The old man kept looking across the dark water. He said nothing. His hand held the motor arm that steered her to freedom.

"Will I make it?" she said half aloud. There was no one to talk to except the old man. And he was silent.

1. At the beginning of the story, what is Isabella thinking about?
   - Ⓐ how cold the river water is
   - Ⓑ how small the boat is
   - Ⓒ how silent the old man is
   - Ⓓ the sound of the small motor

2. Why did she sleep in the woods?
   - Ⓐ because it was warmer there
   - Ⓑ because the bed was too small
   - Ⓒ because soldiers were looking for her
   - Ⓓ because there were no hotels

GO ON →

3. The story never says so, but you can conclude that _____

  Ⓐ the old man is running away.

  Ⓑ the old man is her father.

  Ⓒ she is running from the soldiers.

  Ⓓ she is on a vacation.

4. If this were the beginning of the story, what would you need to know soon?

  Ⓐ who the old man is

  Ⓑ why Isabella is running away

  Ⓒ the name of the little boat

  Ⓓ why it is so cold

5. Guess why the old man drops her suitcase in the water.

  Ⓐ It is dangerous.

  Ⓑ He wants to make her angry.

  Ⓒ It is an accident.

  Ⓓ There is too little room in the boat.

6. How do you think Isabella feels in this part of the story?

  Ⓐ afraid

  Ⓑ comfortable

  Ⓒ happy

  Ⓓ angry

7. How does Isabella act when the old man drops her suitcase into the water?

  Ⓐ She is angry.

  Ⓑ She understands.

  Ⓒ She yells.

  Ⓓ She cries.

8. If this were the beginning of the story, what would you think of Isabella?

  Ⓐ She is very brave.

  Ⓑ She is not brave.

  Ⓒ She is silly.

  Ⓓ She is a bad person.

9. How does the old man let Isabella know he isn't mean?

  Ⓐ He says something nice to Isabella.

  Ⓑ He holds out his hand and helps her aboard.

  Ⓒ Isabella smiles at him.

  Ⓓ He hugs Isabella.

10. How does the writer let us know this will be a difficult boat ride?

  Ⓐ Isabella is already soaked with icy water not twenty feet from shore.

  Ⓑ The old man tells Isabella how difficult it will be.

  Ⓒ Isabella is already crying before the boat leaves the shore.

  Ⓓ The motor will not start.

STOP

Number Correct/Total=_____ /10

10 Reading Literature

Appreciating theme and figurative language

A story's **theme** can teach a lesson such as "Honesty is the best policy." A story's theme can also be a **"big idea"** such as "Growing up is sometimes tough."

Most of the time, you **figure out** the theme yourself. You figure out the theme from what you have **read before** and **your own experiences**.

BUILDING MODEL PLANES

Task 1

Read each selection. Then circle the best answers.

The cold North Sea poured into Holland, ruining its crops. Each farmer built walls of earth and sand to save his farm. They called the walls *dikes*, but those dikes didn't last long. Salt water pounded them until they leaked and washed away. Each year some farmers built bigger dikes. Others gave up and let the sea destroy their farms. Finally, the king gathered the people and said, "Let us all work together. Use clay, stones, and bricks to build stronger dikes. If we work together we will beat the sea."

Working together, the Dutch made dikes so big and so strong that the sea could not break through. Across the land everyone had parties to honor themselves for a job well done.

1. The writer doesn't tell you, but you can learn that _____
   A   you can't fight the sea.
   B   hard work can pay off.

2. Another theme you can learn is that _____
   A   there is a strength in numbers.
   B   farmers build dikes.

3. A third theme is _____
   A   always use the best materials.
   B   the Dutch are good at working together.

☞ **Feedback** You can learn three things from this story. One is that *hard work can pay off*. Another is that *there is strength in numbers*. A third theme is *always use the best materials*.

"Hey, Jeff, come play," yelled Tyler.

Jeff looked at his watch. It was 3:15. He had promised his mom he'd take the milk to Aunt Rebe's house right away. But he really wanted to play ball.

"Okay, Tyler," said Jeff, "but I can only play for half an hour."

The game was great. Jeff's team won. Jeff looked at his watch. It said 5:30. He ran to Aunt Rebe's, but no one answered her door. Then he ran home and no one was there. A note on the kitchen table said, "Dear Jeff, Sorry you missed the treat. Aunt Rebe took us to the new movie at the mall. We're going for pizza after the show. Make a sandwich for your supper. Love, Mom"

4. What is this story's theme?

    A Keep your promises.

    B Deliver the milk.

    C Play ball and you'll get better.

My friend has a painting by an elephant. That's right, the painting was made by a big elephant who lives in a zoo. The elephant held the paintbrush in its trunk and painted pretty colors on the paper. It is a beautiful painting, and it cost the friend a lot of money. But who'd ever pay a lot of money when the artist is an elephant?

5. The theme of this story is _____

    A don't pay for pretty pictures.

    B judge the painting, not the artist.

☞ **Feedback** The theme in four is to *keep your promises*. If Jeff had kept his promise, he could have gone to the movies and had pizza. In five, the painting was beautiful. It doesn't matter who or what did the painting. The lesson is *judge the painting, not the artist*.

Stories often have a **problem** that must be **solved**.
In Jeff's story, the problem was to choose between baseball and the promise he had made.
His choice was his **solution** to the problem.
But he made the wrong choice.
Jeff's choice gives you a theme:
"Keep promises you make!"

When you finish reading stories, remember to ask yourself,
"What did I learn from this story?"

Task 2

Read both parts of this African folktale. Circle the best correct answers.

Olorun, the high god, kept everyone happy. No one had less or more than his neighbor. Everyone had the same color hair, skin, and eyes. Everyone had the same good food and houses. Life was good.

When Olorun was making all the people, he dropped a few by mistake. Those people turned out to be a little different. One he dropped landed on his head. He was called Great Thinker. Great Thinker thought long, long thoughts and made long, long speeches. Most people paid no attention to him. They smiled and went on their way.

One day, Great Thinker finished a long thought. Then he gave a long speech. "Why must we all be the same color?" he asked. "Why aren't some of us richer than others? Why can't we all be different?"

He spoke for so long that some people began to listen.

"How nice it would be to have a house that doesn't look the same as everyone else's," grumbled one man. And that's how it began. The more people grumbled, the more they argued with one another. No one had ever argued before. And after arguments came gossip. And after gossip, people became selfish and greedy.

1. What is the problem the writer describes so far?

   A One man was dropped on his head.

   B The man spoke for a long time.

   C People became selfish and greedy.

   D People went into the wrong houses.

👉 **Feedback** This story is really about people everywhere. The main problem in the story is that *people changed from liking each other to becoming selfish and greedy*. Read more to learn what happens when people are selfish and what Olorun's solution is.

Olorun sent his servant to see what was happening on earth. The servant got an earful and an eyeful. "Give me this! Give me that! Give me a bigger house! More corn! More gold! More goats! Give me red hair! More! Better! Different! But just for me!"

"What a mess!" the servant told Olorun when he returned to heaven.

"Okay," said the angry god Olorun. "I'll give them everything they want, but they'll not be any happier a year from now." And sure enough, when the servant returned to earth a year later, things were worse than before.

"It's all your fault," said the first woman who saw Olorun's servant. "You should have told Olorun to give me what I wanted after my neighbor got her wishes, not before. She got three goats, ten gold pieces, and blonde hair. I had asked for only two goats, five gold pieces, and red hair. Now she has more than I have."

"Enough is enough," said angry Olorun. "The people want to be different. I will give them just what they want!" And in a second, Olorun gave people many different languages. Now they could not understand one another at all.

Since then some people have learned their lesson. They work harder to understand one another and live with the differences. For most, though, gossip, greed, and selfishness are still the rule.

2. What is the theme of this story?

   A Selfishness divides people.

   B A little bit of greed is good.

   C Don't send servants to do a god's job.

   D We should all be different.

3. What is another theme you can get from this story?

    A Different languages help us understand one another.

    B Greed is bad.

    C Don't make a powerful person angry.

    D Don't throw rocks in an argument.

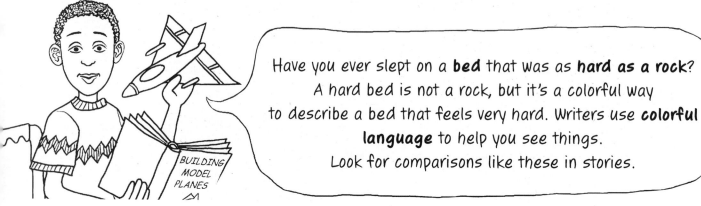

☞ **Feedback** In two, the story's theme is that *selfishness divides people.* In three, another theme you get is that *greed is bad.* (Do you see how stories teach you many things?)

Have you ever slept on a **bed** that was as **hard as a rock**? A hard bed is not a rock, but it's a colorful way to describe a bed that feels very hard. Writers use **colorful language** to help you see things. Look for comparisons like these in stories.

BUILDING MODEL PLANES

Task 3   Circle the best answer.

1. *The clouds sailed across the sky.* Clouds are compared to _____

    A sky.   B cotton.   C sailboats.   D smoke.

2. Why do clouds *sail* and not *jump*?

    A because they are wet   C because they bounce

    B because they leap from   D because they move slowly
       one side to the other   and smoothly

3. Being mean is like sucking on a lemon because _____

    A both make us feel   C both make us happy.
       sour inside.

    B lemons are mean,   D bad people like lemons.
       hard, fruits.

4. *The dry land drank the welcome rain* means that the _____

    A rain was friendly.   C land was like a thirsty person.

    B rain rolled away.   D rain was like a puddle.

☞ **Feedback** In one, clouds remind the writer of *sailboats because they move slowly and smoothly*, the answer to two. A is the answer to three, and the *land was like a thirsty person* is the answer to four.

5. *When I looked at the sky, a million stars winked at me and the moon had a big smile*. The stars are compared to _____

   A mouths.   B diamonds.   C ears.   D eyes.

6. *What a lovely, whispering, tiptoeing day it was*. What kind of day was it?

   A hot   B quiet   C loud   D rainy

7. *Like frozen cotton, the fog lay white, clean, and cold*. These words make you think of _____

   A snow.   B water.   C sun.   D smoke.

8. *The river raced by like a lion*. The river was _____

   A loud.   B quiet.   C wild.   D deep.

9. *The car coughed and sputtered like a sick person*. The car is compared to _____

   A a coffee pot.   C someone with a bad cold.
   B a lawn hose.   D a gas station.

☞ **Feedback** In five, *eyes* can wink and stars can remind us of winking eyes. A whispering day, in six, is very *quiet*. The white fog looks like *snow* in seven. Eight and nine are C and C.

RECAP

You can learn a lot by spotting **themes** in stories. Good writing uses **colorful language** to paint pictures by comparing, for example, a wild river with a wild animal.

See how much you've learned. Take this test.

Questions 1–10. Read the selection. Then choose the best answer to each question. Fill in the circle beside the answer you choose.

The morning sun was peeking from behind a cloud when Alicia suddenly yelled, "Look out for the broken glass!"

But Silly Sam kept his hands in the air and his feet on the handlebars. He heard a sound like stepping on old breadcrumbs, and then the pop of his front tire. Like a jackrabbit, the bike bounced off the path. Sam went flying like a football through the air.

"What now?" Alicia asked. Sam had landed on the sign that said

KEEP OFF THE GRASS.

"What now?" Alicia asked again.

"Now," said Sam, sitting on the sign and studying his flat tire, "now, I take out my ballpoint pen and click the top three times," he said with his best TV cartoon smile.

"Stand back," he warned as he held the pen straight in front of him, as far away as he could. Then he clicked the top three times.

Pow! In a puff of smoke that didn't smell like fire, a huge monster was there.

Alicia screamed. "Look out! What a terrible monster! Run for your life!"

"Stay still, Alicia," said Silly Sam proudly. "Meet my Grubb, my own private Grubb. He belongs to me and only me, and he's my friend. He's everybody's friend." And as he spoke, the Grubb lifted Silly Sam off the sign and put him on the bike path.

A Grubb has an ugly blue face. Its teeth are three feet long, almost as tall as a first grader. Sam's Grubb loves his teeth and brushes them after every meal. He has no nose, but he smells things with his ears. And he is especially good at fixing bikes and caring for silly bike riders. Alicia and Sam were soon on their way home and the Grubb was back in Silly Sam's ballpoint pen.

GO ON

1. What is the main problem in this story?

   Ⓐ Grubbs have ugly faces that scare people.

   Ⓑ Alicia must have a pen that clicks three times.

   Ⓒ Sam has a flat tire and needs it fixed.

   Ⓓ The smoke doesn't smell like fire.

2. What sound does stepping on old breadcrumbs have?

   Ⓐ bang   Ⓒ crunch

   Ⓑ hiss   Ⓓ buzz

3. What makes the sound of stepping on old breadcrumbs?

   Ⓐ Alicia walking over to help Sam

   Ⓑ the tire rolling over the broken glass

   Ⓒ the Grubb coming out of the smoke

   Ⓓ the three clicks of the ballpoint pen

4. What is the theme of this story?

   Ⓐ Don't go out without your ballpoint pen.

   Ⓑ Don't get a flat tire in the park.

   Ⓒ Don't fool around on your bike.

   Ⓓ Don't judge people by their looks.

5. What is another way to state the theme?

   Ⓐ Always ride with someone.

   Ⓑ Don't fear monsters until you get to know them.

   Ⓒ It's good to have a sister.

   Ⓓ Pay attention to what you're doing.

6. What does the writer compare the sun to?

   Ⓐ someone who walks on top of broken glass

   Ⓑ a Grubb without a nose and with long teeth

   Ⓒ someone peeking out from behind something

   Ⓓ a football flying through the air

7. What does the writer compare the bike to when the tire goes flat?

   Ⓐ a football   Ⓒ a pogo stick

   Ⓑ a jackrabbit   Ⓓ breadcrumbs

8. Since no one really has a Grubb, you should learn from this story _____

   Ⓐ to carry a ballpoint pen at all times.

   Ⓑ not to step on the "keep off" sign.

   Ⓒ to be careful when riding bikes.

   Ⓓ to wear seat belts at all times.

9. What kind of smile does Silly Sam have?

   Ⓐ a jackrabbit smile

   Ⓑ a TV cartoon smile

   Ⓒ a Grubb smile

   Ⓓ a football smile

10. How does Silly Sam look when he is flying through the air?

   Ⓐ like a football

   Ⓑ like the sun smiling through clouds

   Ⓒ like a Grubb

   Ⓓ like a jackrabbit

STOP

Number Correct/Total=_____ /10

Keeping Score

Because most standardized tests give your score in both the number correct and in percentages, here's how you can be your own scorekeeper.

- Under the Number Correct, fill in the number of test questions you got right.
- Find the band in the chart below that has the same number of questions that are on your test.
- Follow along the top row of the band to the number of questions you got right.
- Your Percent Score on that test is right below.

		Number Correct	Total Test Items	Percent Score
Test 1	Sounds and Letters		15	%
Test 2	Word Analysis		12	%
Test 3	Word Meaning		12	%
Test 4	Synonyms and Antonyms		10	%
Test 5	Sentence Clues		15	%
Test 6	Main Idea and Details		8	%
Test 7	Constructing Meaning		10	%
Test 8	Evaluating Information		10	%
Test 9	Characters and Plot		10	%
Test 10	Reading Literature		10	%

Total Test Items

8

1	2	3	4	5	6	7	8
13%	25%	38%	50%	63%	75%	88%	100%

10

1	2	3	4	5	6	7	8	9	10
10%	20%	30%	40%	50%	60%	70%	80%	90%	100%

12

1	2	3	4	5	6	7	8	9	10	11	12
8%	17%	25%	33%	42%	50%	58%	67%	75%	83%	92%	100%

15

1	2	3	4	5	6	7	8	9	10	11	12
6%	13%	20%	26%	33%	40%	46%	53%	60%	66%	73%	80%

13	14	15
86%	93%	100%